Teaching
Reading and Writing
Together
THE CLASSROOM CONNECTION

Teaching Reading and Writing Together

THE CLASSROOM CONNECTION

Carl B. Smith
Indiana University

Karin L. Dahl
University of Cincinnati

TEACHERS COLLEGE PRESS

Teachers College, Columbia University
New York and London

Published by Teachers College Press, 1234 Amsterdam Avenue, New York, N.Y. 10027

Library of Congress Cataloging in Publication Data

Smith, Carl Bernard.
  Teaching reading and writing together.

  Includes bibliographies and index.
  1. Language arts (Elementary)   I.   Dahl, Karin L.,
1938–   II. Title.
LB1576.S59   1984   372.6   84-2522

ISBN 0-8077-2736-9

Manufactured in the United States of America

89 88   3   4   5   6

CONTENTS

Acknowledgments   viii
Introduction   ix

1. **The Reading-Writing Connection**   1
   The Connection Unfolds   1
   Language Becomes Concepts   4
   Linking Through the Curriculum   6
   Processing Information for a Purpose   14
   Suggested Readings   18

2. **Motivating Children to Read and Write**   19
   Teachers as Role Models   20
   Parents as Role Models   23
   Literature as a Model   25
   Motivating Students Through Experience Stories   27
   Motivating Students Through Their Interests   31
   Rewards as Motivators   37
   Sharing Motivational Ideas   39
   References   41
   Suggested Readings   42

3. **Learning to Listen**   43
   The Act of Listening   43
   Listening Experiences That Stimulate Writing   48
   Teaching Students to Listen to Directions   52
   Teaching Students to Listen Critically   56
   References   60
   Suggested Readings   60

4. Problems with Words: Phonics and Spelling   **61**
   A Strategy for Unknown Words   62
   Graphemic Base Technique   63
   Phonics Technique   65
   Sound-Spelling Patterns   70
   Visual Sense in Spelling   73
   Practice Writing and Spelling   74
   Reference   77
   Suggested Readings   77

5. Vocabulary Instruction   **78**
   Capturing Interest in Vocabulary Learning   78
   Presenting Words in Context   79
   Providing a Variety of Experiences   82
   Making Words Easy to Remember   83
   Increasing Vocabulary Independently   86
   Using Prefixes, Suffixes, and Root Words in Vocabulary
      Building   89
   Reference   92
   Suggested Readings   92

6. Basic Comprehension   **93**
   Teaching Reading Comprehension   93
   Finding the Main Idea   95
   Teaching Recall of Details   99
   Helping Fluent Readers Retain Information   104
   Teaching Sequence of Events   105
   Summarizing Information   108
   Reference   110
   Suggested Readings   110

7. Critical Thinking in Reading and Writing   **111**
   Fostering Critical Thinking   111
   Teaching Students to Make Inferences   115
   Teaching Students to Draw Conclusions   117
   Teaching Students to Distinguish Between Facts and
      Opinions   120
   Teaching Students to Compare and Contrast Information   123
   Understanding Cause-and-Effect Relationships   126
   Suggested Readings   129

8. Study Strategies: How to Learn and Study Effectively **130**
   Learning How to Learn   130

Following Directions   134
Learning How to Study   137
Suggested Readings   143

9. Teaching Written Composition   **144**
   Elements in Teaching Written Composition   144
   A Basic Strategy for Teaching Composition   148
   Sequence and Development in Children's Writings   150
   Suggested Readings   159

10. Proofreading and Revising   **160**
    Getting Students to Revise   160
    Proofreading Strategy   162
    Group Approach to Proofreading   163
    Teaching from Student Compositions   168
    A Teacher Notation System   170
    Developing a Spelling Consciousness   171
    Making Students Conscious of Capitalization and
       Punctuation   173
    Legibility and Handwriting Style   175
    Rewriting and Revising Compositions   179
    Evaluating Compositions   182

Appendices
    A. Word Parts: Latin and Greek Roots and Prefixes   184
    B. Frequent Phonograms: Vowels and Consonants   187
    C. Phonics Generalizations   189
    D. Phonics Vocabulary   191

Index   **193**

ACKNOWLEDGMENTS

Numerous children's compositions used in this book were selected from those submitted anonymously in a national study of children's compositions.[1] Any personal names that appeared in those compositions were simply changed to letters of the alphabet, thus eliminating the possibility that particular individuals might be identified. The names of the writers were never requested, and so each writer is identified only by a number assigned for computer analysis.

We are able to identify some children by name because separately they sent us compositions or poems. Their names appear with their work within the text and are used with permission.

Ideas for teaching stem from a variety of sources: classroom observations, reading, creative synthesis, and of course from teachers who describe what they do or what they believe is workable. To our associates in teaching and to our students we owe a great debt for their ideas, promptings, and reviews of this manuscript. Teachers who provided particular teaching suggestions include Patricia Ward, Susan Chelminiak, and Janet Hohimer-Hirsch. Special recognition is due Anne Falkner, who provided almost all of the ideas for the second chapter, "Motivating Children to Read and Write." We also thank Deborah M. Abrams, who prepared a number of classroom activities. They are used with her permission.

Others have aided us significantly in this task. Linda Richardson typed and retyped the manuscript. Kerry Kern kept us thinking about our audience with her strong editorial suggestions.

Thank you all for your ideas and encouragement.

---

[1]C. Smith and G. Ingersoll, *The Written Vocabulary of Elementary School Children, Ages 6–14* (Bloomington, Ind.: Education Monographs, Indiana University, 1983).

INTRODUCTION

Linking reading and writing has advantages that push well beyond the fact that they both employ a print medium with similar surface characteristics. They also work with a type of communication more cryptic and formalized than that experienced in oral language. By deliberately tying reading and writing together, the teacher reminds students to learn mutually beneficial aspects of thought and language—vocabulary, organization, phrasing, techniques of clarity and emphasis, and so on. Written language thereby becomes for the student a(language-in-use instead)of being a passive experience of looking at a book.

This book gives classroom strategies and specific activities that tie together reading and writing in a natural way. Strategies and activities are organized around major instructional purposes, as identified through a survey of several hundred classroom teachers conducted by the authors (Smith & Dahl, 1982). Each chapter starts with a brief discussion of one of those purposes, thus enabling us to outline a general strategy for linking reading and writing to achieve that purpose. That initial discussion gives our perspective on the skill or concept and provides a sense of direction to the activities contained therein. It should help teachers decide how to use those activities. It should serve as a procedural framework for teaching the concept or skill and as a guide for teachers in preparing their own original activities.

Ideas to stimulate discussion and interaction are provided throughout the text. They are suggestions to get students involved in thinking about the skill or concept featured in the chapter. Such discussions serve as a means to motivate students and to get them to examine their own ability in the use of the skill under discussion. Also provided are numerous suggested classroom activities designed to help students achieve fluency in the skills being discussed. These classroom-tested activities bring together reading and writing in mutually supportive ways under the topic of the chapter.

Chapter 1, "The Reading-Writing Connection," provides an explanation and examples of how reading and writing are similar and mutually supportive in language, in information processing, and in their instructional steps.

Chapter 2, "Motivating Children to Read and Write," suggests that teachers, parents, and literature provide models to imitate, and that rewards and involvement will stimulate children's interests in reading and writing.

Chapter 3, "Learning to Listen," describes techniques for attending to communications, following directions, and listening with a critical attitude.

Chapter 4, "Problems with Words: Phonics and Spelling," encourages the use of sound-spelling patterns as ways of solving word problems in reading and in writing.

Chapter 5, "Vocabulary Instruction," emphasizes the need to systematically develop one's vocabulary through interest and the use of context, associations, and root words.

Chapter 6, "Basic Comprehension," presents a variety of activities for finding, remembering, and summarizing ideas. New association techniques for recalling details are also included.

Chapter 7, "Critical Thinking in Reading and Writing," promotes techniques that challenge students to make inferences, draw conclusions, and establish an attitude that reading and writing demand alert thinking.

Chapter 8, "Study Strategies: How to Learn and Study Effectively," teaches children how to practice studying and use reference books, especially dictionaries and encyclopedias.

Chapter 9, "Teaching Written Composition," assumes that children can be taught to write compositions, both through a general strategy and through specific exercises on organization, audience awareness, sequencing ideas, and diagnosing what one has written. Sample composition starters are also included.

Chapter 10, "Proofreading and Revising," fosters the idea that a composition needs to be reviewed before its final submission. Especially important to this chapter is the notion that student compositions can be used as effective tools for teaching proof-reading and revision skills.

REFERENCE

Smith, C. and K. Dahl. *Survey: Language Arts Teachers' Need—1982.* Monograph, Language Studies Department. Bloomington, Ind.: School of Education, Indiana University, 1982.

Chapter 1

THE READING-WRITING CONNECTION

(Those who read well usually write well; those who write well generally read well.) You have undoubtedly heard that general statement about the correlation between reading and writing. Speakers and textbooks on language arts often extol the virtues of that correlation, but fail to describe what this means for the practical, everyday activities of the classroom teacher and the child learner. Besides reminding us of something we already know (i.e., those proficient in language are usually proficient in most language tasks), what specifically can a teacher do to link one language activity with another in order to make the learning of both tasks more efficient?

This book describes specific ways to make the connection between reading and writing a valuable daily learning activity for children in the elementary school and in the middle school, grades K–8. It is not meant as merely a list of activities, a sort of file card pile of activities in a book. It translates various abstractions about the reading-writing linkup into instructional strategies and then into sample activities. We feel this approach gives teachers a broad line of reasoning to follow in developing their own activities. We provide sample activities as guides to make our translation more concrete.

THE CONNECTION UNFOLDS

A few activities and a strategy applied to one year in a child's life are not going to make that child an automatic winner in the reading and writing school derby. (The underlying structures and mechanisms for reading and writing are language and thought patterns.) They are developed gradually, across years. So too are reading and writing skills developed, as are children's realizations of how these elements mutually support one another.

An example or two may clarify what we mean by this connection and help illustrate what we mean by the gradual development that is inherent in growth in language and thought. A few years ago we read a newspaper column in which the columnist described a world-wandering acquaintance who wrote short stories that he submitted to various magazines for publication. This wanderer submitted stories for over twenty years without once getting a story published. The columnist commented that writing those stories apparently satisfied a need in his acquaintance—perhaps a need simply to keep a record of his thoughts as he traveled—yet he must surely have wondered from time to time why twenty-plus years of writing had produced no public interest in his ideas. The trouble was, said the columnist, that the man wrote without ever reading. He never read the magazines to which he addressed his stories. He had no sense of style, length, tone, construction, topic, or audience. He simply wrote and mailed his stories to any magazine that had his attention that day. "How," queried the columnist, "could anyone write intelligently without first reading something of similar intent?"

While (reading provides specific facts for writing,) it more importantly provides a writer with a sense of how to communicate in writing. From a teacher's perspective, that general connection needs to become more directive.

Another example comes from a letter we received from an eighth grader named Kathy. Because we are associated with children's books we often receive letters from children. Kathy wrote to us about a mini-mystery from one of our books. This mystery is typical of short sleuth stories. It describes several people who have reason to commit a crime, the crime, and a potential victim. The crime is then committed, after which the reader is led through a solution process. What is different about our mini-mystery, however, is that it stops with the crime and then asks the reader to write a solution to the story.

Kathy is concerned with Mrs. Underwood, a wealthy lady who had numerous hanger-on relatives waiting peevishly for their share in her estate. One morning Mrs. Underwood is found dead in front of an open refrigerator. The story stops and the students are asked to write an ending. Here is the correspondence:

Dear Carl B. Smith:

We have been reading your mini-mystery about Mrs. Underwood. Each member of the class developed his own ending, and we shared them and voted on the best one. That was fun, but now we want to know what the real ending is. Please hurry a response to us because we are waiting anxiously.

My response:

Dear Kathy:

Each of you already has the "real" ending. The real ending is the one that each of you constructed in your own mind. The Underwood mystery was written as an unfinished story. It was designed to make you both reader and writer. You all did a terrific job, especially since you analyzed your endings and voted on the best in the class. Please send it to me so I will know what the "real ending" is.

That correspondence reveals many things about the instructional relationship between reading and writing. It all started with a reading (or did it start with the writing of the unfinished mystery?), which needed some formulation in writing, which led to more thoughtful reading, which prompted curiosity, which led to writing a letter to a very specific audience, who read it, which led to more writing, which led to. . . (Thinking, constructing, language solutions, testing ideas: those processes bring reading and writing together.

Readers are actively involved in(constructing meaning)— Kathy's class, as writers, constructed an ending—and they are naturally curious about the fit of their ideas with the author or with their peers. They need to constantly check the reality of their ideas—Where do I fit? Are my ideas like those of others?

Kathy's classmates wrote conclusions that had value in their written forms. When their ideas became written, they could compare their concepts and their structure with the original or with each other. Their thoughts have taken shape and can be examined either as shaped thought or as clever language—and so can the selection that stimulated their discussion. The teacher has the opportunity of asking the students about the language of the "best" ending to see if it was also a good match with the beginning of the story.

Through writing about reading students become interested in the act of reading and in the act of writing. Because their thoughts take shape, in a sense become concrete, they can say, "Ah, it is OK, but is it the best?"

Kathy's initial letter and our initial response were the first of five exchanges, all about writing and reading. It piqued Kathy's interest about the way authors build their ideas. Each question Kathy raised was answered with a problem not unlike that of putting an ending to the Underwood mini-mystery. We asked Kathy to construct the beginning to the last part of an essay that we sent to her. When she sent in her effort, we sent her the original essay. In another instance we asked her to construct the data that would enable a person to make certain conclusions.

In order to write a reasonable response to our requests, Kathy had to become a different kind of reader from her usual self. She admitted it. She had to think of her reading as an opportunity to formulate ideas, not merely as a chance to act like a sponge and "soak it up." The major connection between reading and writing is the constructive mechanism in the mind that acknowledges both the form and substance of what is being read or written. And so the basic strategy that emerges is: *Be a reader as you would be a writer.* But we cannot stop with a generalized dictum, even though it is the mind and the heart of the connection. Language concept development, information processing, and an instructional process for reading and writing have to be given bones and flesh in order to give teachers and students a clearer sense of how the reading-writing connection works.

LANGUAGE BECOMES CONCEPTS

Language reveals to us the ideas we possess. Reading and listening enable us to expand our ideas. Writing and talking enable us to show and reconstruct ideas. In other words, we build our ideas by reading and by putting those ideas into our own words.

Why have teachers asked students to discuss assigned reading selections? Not to see if they remember all the details. Details can always be searched out when needed. Discussion is necessary to help readers formulate concepts, to see if they were thinking while reading and can now make comprehensible statements about that reading. (Writing some brief summary or reaction often is a better way to start a discussion than just asking for random oral comments. The written exercise helps each individual probe his or her concepts by putting them into language.)

Writing helps children appreciate the words and style of the author they are reading, and summaries or reactions can quickly indicate whether or not the author and reader were communicating. If not, the teacher can adjust instruction to overcome the problem. One of the tasks of a teacher, of course, is to find or adapt instructional reading to the level of development of the child.

Ray Bradbury, a science fiction writer (*Fahrenheit 451*), is said to believe that the best U.S. writer was Edgar Rice Burroughs, author of the Tarzan novels. His reason was that Burroughs could capture the imagination of young and old in language they could appreciate. He would lead them into adventures where good and evil clashed and the reader came away feeling refreshed and rewarded. Few writers have that skill—even fewer textbook writers. All the more reason, therefore, to give students an opportunity to pause and make sure that they have some concepts that they can verbalize.

► **ideas for student discussion and interaction**

Students should routinely write a summary or concept paragraph after reading. Encourage them to use some of the important vocabulary (concepts) that they have learned in their reading. Instead of a summary, a reaction is also appropriate, for example, ask them to describe the mood of the story, or explain it to a friend in another class.

► **suggested activity**

LISTEN AND CHECK.   After students have written a brief summary or reaction to a class assignment, have them underline the major ideas they think their paragraph contains. As some individuals in the class read their paragraphs, the listeners can put a check mark next to their major ideas that also occur in others' paragraphs. Those remaining unchecked could be offered for discussion.

LINKING THROUGH THE CURRICULUM

Unless specific attempts are made to tie reading and writing in the curriculum, most of what has been said in the previous paragraphs will remain fairly general notions that teachers may apply in a random fashion. In the following paragraphs we will outline a framework that an individual teacher or a school system might use to give direction to the mutual support that reading and writing (in fact all communication modes) can supply one another.

If we could agree that language arts instruction is concerned primarily with communication, it would therefore seem beneficial for teachers and students to direct their attention to such things as reading and writing short stories or essays as demonstrations of their competence, just as a swimmer uses the race as a demonstration. Swimmers endure grueling practices because they lead to a race. The same is true in communication. Students will endure grammar, spelling, and decoding activities when they see that those exercises enable them to communicate more effectively, that is, to tell stories, listen and outline, write letters, read books, and so on, more effectively. Thus by changing the performance target, and the kind of language samples that we measure, we not only make the curriculum more real, but we offer the teacher more flexibility in using practice activities to achieve a real communication goal. The practice activities—grammar, spelling, phonics—are means to the end; they are not the end.

In a communications-oriented curriculum, teachers and children still engage in many of the traditional activities. The major difference lies in a rather clear separation between means and ends, between practice activities and performances that demonstrate communication. The performances are clear indications of an ability to communicate, providing evidence of a growing vocabulary, the use of sentences and longer organized utterances, and the understanding and use of narration and explanatory prose in school and in daily life. To arrive at those ends the teacher and children work with decoding exercises, dictionaries, grammar and usage practice, and reading discussions. Those activities are helpful steps leading toward the targets of communication, and those practice exercises can be tested to assure the children that they are increasing their skills. But the major tests are those that demand use of a whole communication unit. Students can show that they understand a short story, for example, when they can tell one or write one. It is understood, of course, that the language arts curriculum includes much more than is tested, or more than is stated here. The major performances listed here are merely sample achievements that demonstrate a student's progress toward becoming a literate, articulate human being.

Using Target Tasks

One way to develop a language arts curriculum is to turn broad goals into developmental tasks or benchmarks that help teachers, supervisors, and parents monitor the progress that children make. For example, in the lower primary grades, the goal of speaking clearly and effectively is demonstrated in the telling of a personal short story that has defined characteristics. The teacher can evaluate that performance with notations such as: (1) high competence, (2) minimal competence, or (3) needs continuing work.

Any selection of benchmarks requires choices, and those choices obviously include some and exclude other competence indicators that the teacher could measure. As teachers we accept that situation and do the best we can to make our choices workable and acceptable. For example, in the early stages of language arts development, a simple short story could be a benchmark: *The child will be able to tell or write a simple short story*. Implied in that target task is the child's prior ability to listen to and read a short story, as well as identify the characters and their working out of a solution to some problem. The teacher then builds toward that short story task by providing the examples, motivation, and skills the child needs to produce the final product. Whether those activities are speaking in clear utterances, writing sentences, or spelling

Table 1.1
Practices Leading to Writing a Short Story (Lower Primary Grades)

PROCESSING LEVEL	LISTENING	SPEAKING	READING	WRITING
1. Concept vocabulary	Listen for certain words.	Dictate an experience story.	Read back an experience story.	Write (spell) common words.
2. Statements about personal experience	Listen to enjoyable stories about personal experience.	Use personal vocabulary in classwork.	Find statements and paragraphs about personal experiences.	Write sentences with initial and final period or question mark.
3. Providing of details in organized set	Listen for specific information.	Describe places and people who live there.	Read for character and place details.	Write descriptions of people and places.
4. Final target: a basic communication	Listen to and analyze stories that have characters and action.	Tell story with characters and action.	Read and analyze a story with characters and action.	Write a short story with characters and action.

words so others can understand without strain, the teacher uses all the language arts resources available to develop those skills for the student.

A framework for interrelating the language arts can be seen broadly in table 1.1. Since the target is to listen to, tell, read, and write a short story, the teacher and the child can see their progress (vertically, reading down) and can also see relationships that transfer learning from one subject heading to another (reading across).

Suppose you want to teach primary-grade children to comprehend and write a short story but you are not sure what they do or do not know. How can you outline the various levels on which you may approach the task? Table 1.1 outlines the teaching of a short story by showing various entry points: vocabulary development, personal experience statements, sequence of events, and the basic communication. Related activities can center on vocabulary development as preparation for reading or writing a short story, all the way to using an entire story as a complete communication. By moving horizontally at level 1, a teacher could read a story or certain sentences, directing the students to listen for certain kinds of words) or to listen for the ways in which particular words are used. The teacher could then ask the children to dictate stories using words that seem to fit the subject of their story. The teacher or an aide transcribes the statements, after which each child shares it with another student or with a small group. This gives the student a chance to see if the selected vocabulary communicates as intended. The final activity in level 1 should enable the child to write the words he has been practicing across listening, speaking, and reading activities. Depending on the child's needs, the writing activity at level 1 may include a spelling exercise.)

If the teacher decides to enter the outline at level 4, all the listening, speaking, reading, and writing activities use complete stories. Between levels 1 and 4 are intermediate levels: using vocabulary in sentences associated with a personal experience and writing descriptions of people and places to gain a sense of order and sequence in narrative writing.

Table 1.1 is not intended to serve as a lesson plan; rather, it is a broad outline showing related language arts tasks that move toward the goal of understanding and producing a short story with character and action. As outlined, it would be appropriate for primary-grade children as well as intermediate-grade children.

Major Communication Functions

The following list contains the major communication functions for an elementary student in terms of writing or producing a communication; the receiving or reading of the communication is implied:

1. Tell a story
2. Give a personal message
3. Present someone's life story
4. Convince someone of a point of view
5. Explain a personal discovery, or the discovery of someone else
6. Describe a scene or an event
7. Apply for a position or license
8. Express personal feelings

9. Give a formal message
10. Explain an idea or process
11. Explore ideas in an organized way

A curriculum that focuses on communication would evaluate its success on evidence that a student can read and write in each function or is at least making continuing progress across those functions.

Primary- and Intermediate-Grade Communications

The following list contains the major benchmarks or products that students may use to communicate. The entries are divided into those that are more likely associated with the primary grades and those more likely associated with the intermediate grades.

Primary	*Intermediate*
personal letters	formal letters
simple stories and puppet show dramas	complicated stories and TV dramas
autobiographies	historical biographies
simple poetry	various poetic forms
descriptions of events (personal journal)	explanations
opinions	arguments and propaganda
reporting	research report
applications and forms	newspaper ads and forms
nonverbal communication (picture books)	nonverbal communication (symbols and body language)

Each of these examples could be organized into an instructional outline similar to the one presented in table 1.1. For any of these target communications, the teacher should start the student at a task or level of development where he can make progress. The older the student the more likely he will be working on several communication targets within the same period of time, for example, a grading period. When reading, he performs the target task and checks it off his own personal checklist. As he works to achieve the target communications, he practices the mechanics and skills that enable him to demonstrate his competence. Those skills may be tested at the discretion of the teacher. For some children a test in itself constitutes effective motivation. But the actual test lies in the challenge to write a message that another person will read and respond to.

The following are sample outlines of several elementary school communication tasks arranged to display a vertical instructional development and to show mutually reinforcing tasks horizontally. The title of the targeted communication is given at the top, and the final exercise at the bottom is that same targeted communication.

Table 1.2 suggests four levels of activity in leading students to an understanding of how to express their opinions in a public forum, such as a schoolroom. The teacher selects an entry point that matches the understanding of the student. This arrangement enables two helpful views of a student related to her performance on "expressing an opinion." A horizontal view (listen, speak, read, write) shows whether she is keeping pace in all areas, or whether

Table 1.2
Expressing an Opinion

LISTEN	SPEAK	READ	WRITE
1. Identify difference between fact and opinion.	State a feeling about an issue or a book. State facts on an issue or book.	Read a belief and fantasy and identify it as an opinion.	List feelings on a given topic. List facts on a given topic.
2. Separate facts and feelings in an opinion statement.	Present feelings and facts in an order that expresses your opinion	Read factual selection and discuss its actuality.	On an issue (or book) write a summary of your opinion.
3. Identify the main idea of an opinion statement.	Practice making opinion statements in class.	Read brief opinion statement, such as a letter to the editor.	In an organized way, write an opinion on some issue or book.
4. Tell the facts and feelings used to support an opinion.	In an organized way, present opinion using feelings and facts.	Read a book review or other opinion essay and separate fact and opinion.	In an organized way, write an opinion on some issue or book.

upper

Table 1.3
Description of People, Things, and Events

LISTEN	SPEAK	READ	WRITE
1. Attend to the reading of appropriate prose and poetry, and discuss the reading of descriptive sentences by peers.	Give one sentence description of a sensory action or general emotional feeling or experience using one or more descriptive words.	Read sentences or brief poems describing a sensory action, or emotional feeling or experience using one or more descriptive words.	Write one sentence or brief poem describing a sensory action or emotional feeling or experience using one or more descriptive words.
2. Attend to the reading or speaking of jingles, poetry, and prose from writings of pupils, children's classics, and appropriate adult literature and discuss personal reaction to descriptive words and phrases.	Organize and present a description of an event, object, or place using action, emotion, and sensory experience words.	Read jingles, poetry, and prose descriptions and include those written by peers. Locate descriptive word(s), phrase(s), and sentence(s).	Write three or more sentences describing a scene, place, object, or event using action, emotion, and sensory words.
3. Attend to the reading or oral presentation of appropriate descriptive prose and poetry from pupils' writings, children's classics, and adult literature, and identify the kind of description that appears in each.	Select and use a reporter guide (5 W's) to present an organized description using specific and expressive verbs, adjectives, and adverbs.	Read descriptive prose and poetry from pupils' writings, children's classics, and appropriate adult literature and identify the kind of description that appears in each.	Write one or more descriptive paragraphs or poetic verses using a reporter guide for an event using specific and expressive verbs, adjectives, and adverbs.
4. Attend to the reading or oral presentation of prose and poetry; identify the figurative language and the mood created by descriptive words.	Organize and present a description of an object, place, person, or event using figurative language and other descriptive words to create mood.	Read increasingly complex descriptive prose and poetry from pupils' writings, children's classics, and appropriate adult literature and identify figurative language and other descriptive words that create mood.	Organize and write more than one paragraph or poetic verse describing an object, person, or event using figurative language and certain descriptive words to create a mood.

the teacher should spend additional effort in one area. A vertical view, reading down, shows the developmental progress that is expected of a student over the years she is in the elementary school. The total table reminds the teacher that these modes of communication are interrelated even though the activity of the moment may have a limited focus.

Table 1.3 displays an outline composed of four instructional levels. The major communication to be achieved is a description that uses figurative language and mood-setting vocabulary—a communication more appropriate for an upper-elementary student than one in the lower grades. Level 1 operates at the sentence level; level 2 expects more than one sentence; level 3 suggests using the five w's of news reporting (who, where, when, what, why) as a guide to description; level 4 develops a longer description with the use of figurative language and mood words.

Table 1.4 displays an outline composed of four instructional levels. The nature of the task suggests upper elementary students because it asks for an organized report based on collected data,

upper

Table 1.4
Research and Reporting

LISTEN	SPEAK	READ	WRITE
1. Listen to a report and identify bits of information the researcher had to gather for his report.	Identify a topic for gathering information and ways to find information.	Read about researchers or reporters collecting information on topics of interest.	Select a topic for doing research.
2. Listen to and identify important details heard in a report.	Discuss ways of collecting data on a specific topic.	Read a report and determine where the researcher got his information.	Collect data and keep it in an organized way.
3. Listen to and identify the conclusions heard in a factual presentation.	Discuss how to categorize and outline data collected.	Read a report and outline its major categories and conclusions.	Outline the paper and categorize information collected in the outline.
4. Listen to and summarize (retell) the steps the speaker took in presenting a factual report.	Give a presentation of data that provides meaningful information to listeners.	Read a report and tell how to verify its information.	Submit an organized report based on a number of identified sources.

that is, a research report. Level 1 focuses on selecting a workable topic; level 2 on collecting and organizing data; level 3 on outlining a report; and level 4 on producing an organized report based on a variety of sources.

PROCESSING INFORMATION FOR A PURPOSE

(Reading and writing concern themselves with processing information. Whether acting as a reader or writer, the child has to ask himself: How do I take this information and make it meaningful? Central to that question is the guiding role of purpose or intention: (Why am I reading this? or Why do I want to communicate these ideas in writing? It would be helpful if all children had those two questions blazoned on a card in front of them throughout their school careers!

The intention of the reader or writer serves as the primary mechanism for selecting information and for organizing what is selected. After that the ability and skill of the individual determine the outcome, that is, the synthesis that occurs in reading or the composition in writing. If children know that school reading assignments require a retelling of information or events in their stated sequence, that knowledge becomes their guide for selecting and organizing what they will try to retain. In like manner, their writing will tend to list details or events in chronological order with little other thought given to a composition, if that is the kind of processing children associate with school tasks.

Levels of Processing

There are two major ways of analyzing information processing for purposes of instruction. One way looks at the quantity of information to be processed; the other looks at the kind of thinking required to process the information. Regarding quantity, the teacher can ask: Can the child process: (1) the entire selection, (2) a section or a paragraph, (3) a sentence, or (4) the key vocabulary or a word? Diagnostically, the teacher examines the child's performance to see at which quantity level the child can function. If satisfactory responses or performances occur for the entire selection, there is no need to check smaller units. But for some children, even at the upper elementary grades, processing sentences or even the vocabulary poses a problem.

(As an aid to processing information for a written composition, it is often helpful to start by listing words that represent important concepts.) When a group of children is writing on the same subject, listing words on the board gives each of them a set of concepts and a vocabulary that they can start with. After that the children can write single statements that represent some of the major thoughts they have on the subject. Those statements could be shared or tried on a partner as a way of seeing where gaps occur and where help is needed before attempting to organize a coherent message.

The second way to approach information processing is to examine the kind of thinking used to process the information. Certainly there are many types of thinking that could be discussed, but we will restrict them to three types or levels that can guide instruction in reading and writing:

1. Linear thinking that retells a story or a message
2. Interpretive thinking that provides a theme or a moral
3. Evaluative thinking that measures the story against a standard or benchmark

A teacher could demonstrate these levels of information processing by asking children to respond to one of Aesop's fables, for example, the story of the shepherd boy who cried "Wolf!" The three levels of thinking could be observed in an elementary school class by asking these questions:

• Who can retell the story?
• What is the moral of the story?
• Why did the boy and the townspeople act the way they did?

In a similar fashion, a teacher could get children to write and process on any of those levels by directing them to:

1. Write a story that has a clear sequence of events.
2. Write a story that exemplifies a theme or moral.
3. Write a story that shows characters making mistakes or making judgments about something important.

In the composition that follows, a sixth-grade boy gives us a first-draft example of his processing information at his level of evaluative thinking. He wrote:

My Dads

My mom was married when she was 18. Because she was pregnant with my older brother S. When S was about 4 years old B (my dad) used to beat him. And then she became pregnant with me. Which was an accedent. And when I was born B left us. Which really makes me feel good. I have only seen him about 10 times after he left.

Then a couple of years later she married C. I don't really remember that much of him. My mom and brother say he used to beat me. But, he would come home drunk almost every night. And he smoked too. And my mom found out a lot of different but personal poroblems he had. And she could not cope with them. So they were devorced.

I don't know how long it was But then she married D. I didn't like him from the start. He was always mean to my mom, and he tried to hit her with a chair once. Ever since then I've really disliked him. She devorced him.

Then about 2 or 3 years later she married E. I think thats how he spelled his name. I liked him. But just before they were married she found out some personal things about him. She picks some real winners. So she got an annulment.

So she dated for a while. And pretty soon D was back. They dated off and on. One night they went out and when I woke up in the morning she wasn't home yet. Just before I left for school she called and said she was going to pick me up from school. And she told me her and D had got married last night. So there I was stuck with a man I didn't like and my mom was married to him. But pretty soon D was seeing some other girl so they got an annulment.

Now she's dating a lot of guys. And she says she's not going to marry for a long time. And only if its in the temple.

But I don't know what to believe what she says. In a way I think she aught to give up guys.

The value in students and teachers looking at information processing is their realization that processing information is an active, learned behavior. The following paragraphs outline some ways that processing can be approached for reading and for writing.

Common Instructional Steps

processing
ref. - learned
(behav).

In reading instruction, it has been common for teachers to direct reading in three steps: prereading activity, reading for a purpose, and discussion and review. Writing benefits from a similar staging: prewriting, writing with intention, and revising. In each of these steps similar thinking and classroom interaction can occur.

STEP 1: PREREADING/PREWRITING.   Step 1 calls for making associations, drawing on background experiences, calling up vocabulary, and bringing the topic into focus. It may require motivational or interest-raising activities, depending on the children's perception of the topic. The primary objective of this step is to call forth or to develop ideas about a topic and to select those that appear useful for step 2. It involves getting the mind ready. It is a preview.

STEP 2: READING/WRITING WITH INTENTION.   Step 2 calls for reading or writing for personally established purposes. Decisions have to be made about reasons for doing the activity, the intended outcome, and what will guide the mind. The objective of step 2 is to keep the mind focused while reading or writing.

STEP 3: SUMMARIZING AND REVISING.   Step 3 calls for the mind to confirm its work. This may be as simple as summarizing what has been read in order to tie ideas together or rereading what has been written to make sure major points have been made. Step 3 may also involve adjusting previous perceptions into a different set of ideas and revising the written composition in order to have it communicate more effectively with the intended audience.

As an instructional guide these three steps help the teacher teach children a way to manage any communication they care to tackle. It may become a general strategy for use either in reading or writing.

SUGGESTED READINGS

Applebee, Arthur N. "Writing and Reading." *Journal of Reading* 20, no. 6 (March 1977): 534–37.

Moffett, James. "Reading and Writing as Mediation." *Language Arts* 60, no. 3 (March 1983): 315–22.

Wilson, Marilyn J. "A Review of Recent Research on the Integration of Reading and Writing." *The Reading Teacher* 34, no. 8 (May 1981): 891–901.

Chapter 2

MOTIVATING CHILDREN TO READ AND WRITE

I always
   waste time
      I sharpen my pencil
         for spelling,
            Break it to get away
               from reading.
                  Go to the bathroom
                     for math,
                        Drop things
                           for science,
                              But waste no time
                                 for poetry.

Christopher Quigley, Grade 5
(Published by permission.)

Too often we think of motivation as a bag of tricks or group of techniques to grab students' attention rather than a means for tapping the energies of students and keeping them on task. Like the magician on stage, a teacher may enjoy the razzle-dazzle of a bag of tricks, showing up in costume, having surprise guests, or playing rock music as a stimulus for writing, but the teacher's continuing problem is to provide long-term motivation for students.

To promote student interest and commitment the teacher could work on providing stimuli for the classroom and home environments and on highlighting the personal interests of the students. As is only natural, students are influenced by what they see and hear regularly. The teacher's attitudes and actions toward books, for example, gradually affect the attitudes and actions of students. The same is true for parents. Teachers and parents are role models for their children. What they do with books and writing and the experiences they provide gently shape the child's sense of how to respond to books. Literature, or more precisely the books and magazines available to the child, also acts as a model that may influence the future reading and writing habits of children. Perhaps more attention needs to be paid to these influences.

The collective and individual interests of the children must certainly be explored and expanded in any discussion on motivating children to read and write. Personal interests, sometimes partially hidden from the students themselves, are bases from which language activities can proceed.

Role models, literature, and interests are the quiet motivators in a student's world. Less subtle, but still quite effective, are the uses of awards and rewards. Classroom displays of students' work, recognition certificates, and even compliments from the principal show children that their work has some immediate value. These awards can foster a positive attitude in the child, and thus provide support to the overall effort to motivate children to use reading and writing in their lives.

TEACHERS AS ROLE MODELS

Teachers play a critical role in affecting students' attitudes toward reading and writing. Their encouragement and influence help students adopt a positive attitude toward these two processes. As role models, teachers need to be "caught in the act" of reading; they should let students see that they choose to read books and that books are an interesting and important part of their lives. Part of the power of the sustained silent reading programs that have been adopted by many school systems is just that factor: children see their teacher reading (and, for that matter, the principal, secretary, and other staff members).

Similarly, the example of the teacher writing helps to show students that the teacher regards writing as personally important. Teachers can model writing in the classroom by simply writing at the same time that students write in response to an assignment. The teacher can share her piece of writing along with the students, saying, "Here's what I wrote. . . ."

Students, watching this model of teacher as reader-writer, are likely to want to copy it. Even the most reluctant student may think, "Hmm, she's willing to do the assignment, I guess I will too."

Modeling Interest in Reading

Teachers model interest in reading when they read books aloud to the class, something teachers have done for years. Some of the best classroom moments are those shared class experiences where everyone finds out just how sad *Charlotte's Web* is at the end or how funny *Curious George* is in a particular escapade. The implied message in these read-aloud experiences is that the teacher thinks the book (and the act of reading) is interesting, too.

The following special projects and interest centers provide motivation for reading and writing in the classroom and show that the teacher encourages students to participate.

▶ **suggested activity**

CREATE A HIDEAWAY.   Many students are motivated to read and write if they have a quiet retreat. Making room for such a place in a busy classroom is a challenge that classroom teachers meet in some very creative ways. Refrigerator cartons have been turned into space capsules, closets have been converted into mini-vans, and a space behind a filing cabinet has been made homey with a rug, rocking chair, and pillows. The ultimate in seclusion was a "tree house" that, although it lacked the tree, had floors and railings. The effect was an upper level to one portion of the classroom accessible only by ladder. It was designed to be a special hideaway for those needing solitude, quiet, and a place to think.

Another teacher appropriated an old-fashioned bathtub for a reading center. It was painted a bright orange and carried a "No Splashing" sign. The center was full of eager readers at every free moment.

While we are not advocating that the teacher crawl into the tub, we are suggesting that these centers be a place where the teacher also enjoys reading; where (perhaps leaning on the tub) he reads intently from a book that is just right for him.

Fostering Interest in Writing

The following guidelines are designed to help teachers present the task of learning to write creatively in a manner that may instill student interest.

Guidelines for Promoting Creative Writing

1. Emphasize the process rather than the product. Do not cover the students' creative writing efforts with red marks.
2. Create an atmosphere in which students feel free to express themselves openly. Praise their efforts and maintain a positive attitude.
3. Provide opportunities for students to read their work aloud.
4. Be patient with students who are slow starters or disinclined to write.
5. Do not expect the same standard or style of writing from each student.
6. Help students recognize they are writing for a specific audience and see that the paper is delivered to that audience. This tends to improve the quality of writing.
7. Provide a variety of imaginative activities including many open-ended topics that give students the latitude to be creative.
8. Write! Practice what you teach. The teacher becomes a role model.

There are a number of classroom writing centers that teachers and students can enjoy and in which the modeling of interest in writing can take place.

▶ **suggested activities**

THE SUGGESTION BOX.   One teacher put a big suggestion box on a table near his desk. He made an important moment out of the time in the day when he checked for new suggestions, at first looking amazed that none were there (when the program was just getting started) and later showing excitement over finding some suggestions. As the program progressed, he began sharing some of the most interesting suggestions by reading them aloud to the class. These anonymous suggestions provided a vehicle for modeling interest in reading, a real reason for students to engage in writing, and a wealth of colorful suggestions from students.

THE NEWS CENTER.   A news desk can be set up in a corner *news* of the room in which the "editors of the day" are seated. Their job is to receive news items (stories, features, news bulletins) from the class and edit them for a daily news program later in the day. The teacher can submit news times for each program, modeling his interest in writing and in the news project.

A variety of formats can be used for the daily news "broadcasts." Some students present their broadcasts from a desk or lectern in the front of the room, while others sit behind a cardboard T.V. set. On a more elaborate level, students have sought the advice of news experts and used videotape equipment and a television monitor for their productions. Once a week a news summary could be typed by an aide and duplicated for the class and other people in the school.

PARENTS AS ROLE MODELS

Parents generally have an important impact on their children's views on language and on reading and writing in particular. Parents who read and value books themselves, who read to their children, and who take their children to the library can effectively transfer their comfort and interest in reading to their children. Parents who write letters, write notes to family members, or write lists of things to do during a given day are modeling writing at home. The following general suggestions are recommended for parents who want to encourage their children in reading and writing. A teacher may wish to distribute some of these suggestions through a parent newsletter or discuss them at parent-teacher programs.

Guidelines for Parents

1. Have a wealth of printed material available in the home including books, magazines, and newspapers.
2. Set aside a specific time daily to read and write. Let the child see you productively involved in reading-writing activities.
3. Control T.V. viewing versus reading-writing time. Work out a balanced schedule. For every hour of T.V., engage in an equal amount of reading-writing time.

▶ **suggested activities**

In addition to these general suggestions, there are a number of specific activities that parents can do in order to model reading and writing.

SURROUND CHILDREN WITH A VARIETY OF GOOD BOOKS AND PRINTED MATERIAL.   Look for book fairs, book stores, and paperback exchange shops as places to pick up some interesting yet inexpensive reading material. Try lending and exchanging books among friends. Parents may buy a book for themselves and a book for their children.

ENCOURAGE CHILDREN TO WRITE DOWN THEIR REACTIONS TO READING MATERIALS.   Extend the pleasure of a just-read book by providing the child with a brightly colored journal or diary in which private thoughts and feelings concerning the book can be recorded and reactions to characters, events, setting, or the historical perspective can be recounted.

READ ALOUD TO EACH OTHER.   Encourage appreciation of a wide variety of literature and authors by reading aloud selected poems, plays, and short stories. Start with reading and sharing short selections or a chapter a night. Try writing a poem or short play together.

EXPLORE THE LIBRARY TOGETHER.   Knowing what resources are close at hand will encourage use of this facility. Find out the hours, special services offered, and location of favorite sections of books and materials. Most libraries offer a variety of materials for lending, including films, records, and art work. Parents will want to check out books for themselves and show interest in the books and materials children are selecting.

PLAY WORD GAMES TO DEVELOP AND EXTEND VOCABULARY. Obvious choices include ready-made games such as Scrabble, Password, Spill and Spell, Jeopardy, and crossword puzzles. Placing a new word on the message board each day is another way to increase vocabulary. It is the child's responsibility to look up the meaning and try to use it. Discussing the word's meaning each evening and using it in context should help the child to remember the word and make it a part of his or her everyday vocabulary.

WRITE NOTES TO EACH OTHER.   Place notes in a lunch box or a coat pocket, on the bulletin board, or under a pillow. Encourage written responses and keep the dialogue flowing. These interchanges will develop skills in composition and language.

SHARE SECTIONS OF THE NEWSPAPER.   Reading and discussing the daily paper together can serve to advance critical thinking and writing skills. Identify sports articles, comics, movie reviews, or editorials for all to read. Then, discuss your reactions and formulate an opinion on an issue of importance. Help the child to write a "Letter to the Editor" to express his or her view.

LITERATURE AS A MODEL

Typically, when we think of role models, we think of people. But in terms of good language patterns, worthwhile literature becomes an excellent means of presenting learners with powerful role models. It provides examples of the richness of language and presents a wealth of vicarious experience for young learners. Some books provide patterns that children can use in their own stories.

As children listen to good literature read aloud or read it independently, they can be aware that part of what makes these stories special is the language that the author chooses. Some authors find that colorful metaphors are most effective: for example,

"Sliding down the water like a sled on a slippery hill" (Kranz, 1967). Others just make a mood so vivid that children want to jump right into the story. In Maurice Sendak's *Where the Wild Things Are* (1963) the line "Let the wild rumpus begin!" is such a descriptive choice of words.

Good literature abounds with such special moments, and children instinctively are drawn to them. Without belaboring the point or worse, spoiling the story, teachers can emphasize these special moments. Discussion can be stimulated using statements such as, "I think she [the author] said that just right," or "What is your favorite description or favorite passage in this story?"

Children need to be reminded that most of their writing tasks have prototypes or models in the books and magazines they find around them. The poem they want to write, the mood they want to create, or the mystery they want to tell may turn out more to their satisfaction if they try to see how other authors have approached the same problem.

▶ **suggested activities**

The following activities can be used to help students model their writings after other familiar and comfortable forms of literature.

HAVE CHILDREN REFORMAT A SHORT STORY INTO A PLAY.   They should first review books of plays from the library to familiarize themselves with a basic play format.

HAVE CHILDREN WRITE VARIOUS TYPES OF POEMS.   Some poems rhyme, some do not. Distribute a variety of poetic types to the class or have that variety available on a table in the class. After discussing the freedom of poets to express feelings and images, ask the children to write one poem that rhymes and one that does not—perhaps on the same subject. Discuss which they prefer.

HAVE CHILDREN WRITE A PERSONALITY FEATURE STORY ON SOMEONE THEY KNOW.   Feature stories on personalities are popular newspaper and magazine pieces. Have students read several for ideas and approaches. Weekly newspapers and magazines for children (in the library) are excellent resources. Afterward ask the children to prepare a personality feature of their own, perhaps in teams. Disc jockeys, sports figures, singers, actors, local characters, the principal, the custodian, a storekeeper—all are possibilities for this task.

MOTIVATING STUDENTS THROUGH EXPERIENCE STORIES

Being successful in a task is one of the surest ways of motivating someone to want to do the task again.

Children often are successful in their first attempt at reading if they have written the selection themselves, that is, they have dictated it and someone wrote it down. Their attempt to organize their thoughts in writing appears to help children better comprehend works written by others (Platt, 1977). The process of dictating and writing personal experience stories is usually referred to as the language experience approach. Each child's language and experiences are used to create reading material. The student's own writing helps him recognize the connection between oral and written language. The child develops his thoughts on a subject and subsequently verbalizes them. The teacher or child records these thoughts, followed by the child reading the story he has created. The following list outlines this procedure.

How to Build an Experience Story

Gain experience.
Gather and categorize information.
Voice thoughts and ideas.
Record thoughts and ideas as recounted.
Read corrected story.

Types of Experience Writing

The following are different types of personal experience writing exercises arranged in a progression of their difficulty.

LISTING BY CATEGORIES.   The teacher identifies a topic. The students respond with appropriate words for that category. For example, pets: dog, gerbil, goldfish. The teacher records the responses.

DESCRIPTIONS.   The teacher provides a noun and elicits descriptive words from students to enhance the meaning of the noun. For example, tree: green, graceful, glossy-leafed. The teacher records the responses.

SHORT STATEMENTS.   The student gives a sentence in response to an experience on a given subject. For example, the circus: I saw tigers. This is a teacher-directed activity. Either the teacher or student records the responses.

EXPANDED WRITING.   The student is at a more advanced stage and capable of elaborating on a given topic-related experience in a group setting. For example, I saw the striped tigers jump through rings of fire.

INDEPENDENT WRITING.   The student can compose and record his or her own story.

After completing any of these writing exercises, the child who composed the story may read it back and thereby feel successful in reading his own composition. The experience story may also be read by other members of the class, creating the opportunity for discussion and reinforcement.

▶ suggested activities

Children can be involved in developing group experience charts.

ORGANIZATIONAL CHARTS.   Charts are useful in establishing procedures or conveying instructions for classroom activities. Possible topics for these charts include: playground rules, classroom helpers, how to operate the video recorder, the formula for composing a successful story, or how to organize a business letter. Here is a sample for one.

Classroom Helpers

Sharpen pencils.
Water plants.
Clean erasers.

NARRATIVE CHARTS.   The purpose of these charts is to record experiences of the class from field trips, visitors, speakers, films, or outside resources.

Our Trip

We went to the airport.
We saw planes in many shapes
sizes and colors.
It was fun to go up in the
control tower.
We saw planes on radar.
We watched some planes take off
and saw others land.

GROUP EXPERIENCE STORIES.   These work well with beginning readers in the early primary grades. The teacher must be skillful in guiding the selection of topics. Pets, trips, news events, or pictures can be used as focal points for discussion. Building common experiences is an important factor. The most imaginative productions are achieved with a teacher who frees children to express themselves naturally, using the child's language without trying to structure it according to the teacher's standards.

The following episode shows how one teacher set the stage for a classroom writing activity. The first-grade teacher had gone to the supply closet in the room to pull out some sheets of art paper. As she reached into the farthest corner, she brushed against other items stacked in the closet. The items shifted and the movement suprised her. She jumped, but not nearly so far as the tiny gray mouse who was peering out from an old bird's nest on the shelf. The mouse ran, the teacher screamed, and pandemonium reigned. The teacher decided to turn the incident into a learning experience. The children were delighted since they all had experienced the mouse firsthand. He instantly became the classroom celebrity. Ideas were plentiful, and interest and enthusiasm ran high. Here is the spontaneous experience chart story that resulted.

Our Mouse

A mouse came in our room today.
It was funny.
Everyone was surprised.
The mouse was in our closet.
He had a home in there.
His home was in a bird's nest.
We wanted him to stay.
He ran away.

READING CHARTS.   Charts may be developed as part of reading lessons to teach, reinforce, or review specific skills or understandings. They can be developed in conjunction with vocabulary, comprehension, or study skill activities. The following two examples are geared toward providing children with an opportunity to apply their reading skills.

"Ch" Words

Charlie and the children changed to chopsticks to eat their Chinese chicken dinner. We chuckled at Charlie as he chased the chopped-up chicken off the china onto the chair. Chopsticks proved quite a challenge to Charlie.

Find the Root Word

thoughtful   trainable
donation   unruly
reviewing

PERSONAL EXPERIENCE STORIES.   Pleasant experiences with group authorship often lead individuals into composing their own experience stories. This is a record of the child's own experience using his language. Pictures are often used to add interest and enhance understanding of the story when it is read by the child and others. The individual stories usually represent greater personal involvement and familiarity with the topic.

My Pets

We have two cats.
They are brown and white.

They like to play outside.
Their names are Phoebe and Mitsu.

MOTIVATING STUDENTS THROUGH THEIR INTERESTS ✓

Children will read and not put the work aside if the story strikes a chord within them. Just as the author works with a specific purpose and audience in mind, so the child needs a personal reason or a specific purpose for becoming a good communicator. The functional as well as the fun side of reading and writing must be revealed to the child, thereby making these activities not only school tasks but also means to express feelings, to participate in adventure, to satisfy curiosity, to solve a problem, and so on.

Teachers can help children use their interests by watching what books students select, what subjects or topics they concentrate on, and what categories of information they discuss. The original writing of students will often indicate personal preferences.

▶ **ideas for student interaction and discussion**

Children's experiences can lead to personal interests. Use a group experience as a means for discussing how those experiences can prompt a search for information through reading and a sharing of information through writing. For example, arrange for students to spend a day in court observing a trial that has interested them. Have students search out and study articles from newspapers and magazines about a particular case being heard. Ask students to take a side, either pro or con, and present arguments to support their position. Their arguments or reasons must be written in advance of a follow-up discussion on the case. Discuss the judicial process and the checks and balances that are built into our judicial system. Discuss the possible misconceptions they may have based upon the way the judicial system is presented in courtroom scenes on television.

Ask the students if any of them became interested in the courts and our legal system as a result of this activity. Point out that personal interests usually develop as the result of a good experience. People expand their interests as they reach out for broader experiences. Discuss with them the fact that a true interest usually involves spending time to learn more about it.

✓ Interest Inventories

Sometimes students are unaware of their own interests. An interest inventory is one way to help children find their interests. A movie, poster, game, or simply a friend's prodding may also serve as a catalyst. Interest inventories come in all lengths and types. The examples shown in figures 2.1 and 2.2 have proven effective with elementary students. Teachers frequently use these inventories to become better informed about their students. Teachers can construct their own inventories to reflect materials available in the classroom, the school library, or current units of study.

A pie-shaped chart labeled according to interest categories is another way to indicate students' preferences (see figure 2.3 on page 34). When a student reads a book or writes a theme on a self-selected topic, he writes the title and author in the appropriate category of the chart. At a glance, the teacher or student can see if there are patterns of interest.

Figure 2.1
Inventory of Reading and Writing Interests

Complete the following sentences. Please respond freely.

Reading is _____

Writing is _____

I would read more often if _____

_____

I would write more often if _____

_____

I enjoyed reading _____

I enjoyed writing _____

I like to read when _____

I like to write when _____

I'd rather read than _____

I'd rather write than _____

_____

Figure 2.2

Inventory of Reading and Writing Habits and Interests

Please answer the following questions.

1. Do you have books of your own? How many?

2. Do you read to or with someone at home?

3. What do you like to read about?

4. What is the title of your favorite book?

5. What do you read besides books?

6. What would make you want to read more often?

7. What would encourage you to write more often?

8. Do you have a place where you can go to write or to read?

9. What kind of writing do you like to do?

10. If you were to write your own book what would you write about?

TOPICS OF INTEREST TO PRIMARY STUDENTS.   The following are some categories that have held appeal for primary-aged students.

pets	sci-fi	playing
games	friends	family
T.V.	bikes	school

TOPICS OF INTEREST TO INTERMEDIATE STUDENTS.   Intermediate and junior high students are often interested in the following categories.

entertainers	super heroes	collections
cars, vans	sports	fashion
motorcycles	music	computer games

Figure 2.3
Pie Chart Interest Inventory

Write the names of books (and authors) in the appropriate spaces. List your own original writing, too. Make your own categories in the blank areas.

▶ **suggested activities**

POPULAR SONGS.   Have students bring in the lyrics to a song they enjoy. It should be a ballad or a song that tells a story. The lyrics from a popular song can be used to provide the basis for a poetry lesson. Although not all music has suitable lyrics, the works of artists such as Judy Collins, Harry Chapin, or John Denver can provide strong examples of visual imagery and an opportunity to analyze the lyrics at an interpretive level. Suggest that students paraphrase the lyrics and then sing (or read) the song to the class.

They might add a verse or two to extend the ballad or change it to suit their imagination.

BOOK OF RECORDS.   Use of the *Guinness Book of World Records* can stimulate excitement among even the most reluctant learners. Focusing on the student's favorite sport or athlete, for example, can provide the preliminary information needed to launch a mini-project on a "student-selected" topic. Helping that student to use additional resources from the library will enable him to realize the vast amount of information available to him and teach him how to use this to his best advantage. For example, one child might develop a background profile on track star Wilma Rudolph and read a brief summary to the class. The report could be a means for prompting related summaries by encouraging a "web of interest" to provide subtopics within a theme that interests members of the group (Norton, 1977).

By drawing a web diagram on the board, the teacher could fill in sections as students express an idea or an interest in some aspect of the subject. Each student can write a summary paragraph on one aspect. The combined report develops some interesting facts and ideas on the theme. See figure 2.4 for a sample of a completed web diagram.

Figure 2.4
Web of Interest

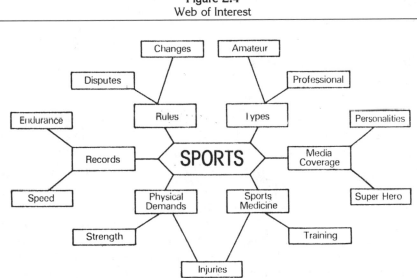

COLLECTIBLES.   Most children delight in collecting items. The collections may range from hot wheels to decals to seashells to cassette tapes. Children can be encouraged to expand their collections by reading about sources for additional items and then writing away to obtain them. Children themselves are often the best source for eliciting suggestions concerning intriguing collections. Encourage all members of the class to start a collection. Have the class develop a list of things to collect.

baseball cards
dolls
stamps
autographs
leaves/seeds
jokes/riddles
poetry
photographs
figurines/knick-knacks
tv scripts
books (mysteries, historical novels, biographies)
scrapbooks (about me, my family, my favorite TV star)

postcards
matchbooks
rocks
buttons/badges/patches
logos
coins
comic books
crayon rubbings (historical sites, graveyards)
posters
memorabilia from a certain era or theme (1920s, Coca Cola)
stuffed animals
video, electronic, or computer games
newspaper clippings (historical events, sports heroes)

In recognition of students' varied collections, a hobby fair could be organized as a culminating activity. An event such as this would give students the opportunity to display their collections and write an explanation of how to start others like them.

TV CRITIC.   Let students sign up for their favorite television program and write a synopsis after viewing it. Discuss what a critic's job entails and have students develop a list of questions to answer as they write about their program. Post the reviews on a bulletin board for others to read.

COMPUTER BUG.   The computer is an excellent resource for a variety of creative activities related to reading and writing. In schools with computer labs for students, almost everyone would enjoy using the word processing capability of the computer for editing and rewriting a short communication before seeing it printed by the computer's printer. Some computer-wise students may want to try their hand at developing a new video game.

CALENDAR RIDDLE.   Have students develop a riddle that reveals its clues day by day on the week's calendar. Each day, place a clue in the appropriate day's square. A student may write only one guess for the week. The actual solution is pasted in on the weekend for review the following Monday.

Clues

Sunday: Sky
Monday: I am large and have all colors in me.
Tuesday: I need both sun and rain to exist.
Wednesday: I am shaped like an arc.
Thursday: Famous songs have been written about me.
Friday: You might find a pot of gold at one end of me.
Saturday: I'm a RAINBOW.

REWARDS AS MOTIVATORS

We always are pleased when we win an award or when our efforts to achieve and excel are recognized either extrinsically, as when an honor student wins a scholarship, or intrinsically, as when a teacher feels a sense of attainment because a student finally managed to write a coherent paragraph.

We start rewarding children at an early age—an ice cream cone for being good, a gold star for an excellent paper. Children usually respond well to this form of motivation and recognition.

Young Authors

A Young Authors Program combines intrinsic and extrinsic rewards by combining bookmaking with creative writing. Children are given the opportunity to write and bind their original works. They then exhibit them at book fairs and shopping centers so that others can read and enjoy their work. Certificates are often awarded to each participant. By seeing the fruits of their labors published in book form, the student writers feel a real sense of personal accomplishment, and the experience may have a highly positive impact on the value they place on communication and self-expression. Through this early positive experience with writing and books, children can develop an interest and sensitivity that can be nurtured throughout their educational experience and life. The following is a blue ribbon winner in poetry.

Leaves

Leaves.
In the trees.
All around the yard.
At the park.

Like

Blowing kites.
A rainfall in the spring.
A picture

Falling

To the streets.

Mark Shumaker, School 107, Indianapolis Public Schools
(Published by permission.)

▶ **suggested activities**

Children's writing can receive recognition and encouragement in many ways. The following list contains examples of activities to help motivate young authors.

1. Let children go into other classrooms to read a few passages from their own books to stimulate other students' interest.
2. Have children write and conduct a sixty-second book review on the public address system.
3. Encourage children to make book mobiles about their own story.
4. Hold autograph parties with young authors. Invite an adult author of children's literature to participate.

5. Have a dress-up day when children can come dressed as a character from their own book.
6. Have a contest to design a reading"mascot" for the Young Authors Program.
7. Design a costume to be worn by the mascot so that anyone donning the costume can promote the Young Authors Program at any time throughout the year.
8. Publish a newsletter featuring current projects and activities concerning the Young Authors Program. Print letters from young authors.
9. Compile recipes from young authors into an authors' cookbook.
10. Make bookmarks and badges for the Young Authors Program.
11. Create a logo for the Young Authors Program that can be duplicated on certificates of accomplishment, stickers, awards, balloons, and so on.

SHARING MOTIVATIONAL IDEAS

One of the richest sources of motivational ideas for relating reading and writing is your fellow teachers. In the teachers' lounge you can agree informally to share one idea a week. If the sharing group were only three or four teachers, that would give you two or three ideas a week to choose from—one hundred ideas a year.

The OMAR Program

A group of teachers from Evansville, Indiana, focused on creating an awareness among students and teachers of quality children's literature. The result was a program that motivates students to read and write about good books. The OMAR (Omar Makes Avid Readers) program,[1] as it is called, is a takeoff of the national Newbery Award. In this case, rather than a panel of distinguished educators voting a best-book award, the children themselves read and judge which of a selected group of books are winners.

---

[1]For more information, write OMAR, Evansville-Vanderburgh School Corporation, Reading Center, 1 S.E. Ninth Street, Evansville, IN 47708 (telephone 812-426-5060).

A number of motivational activities including bookmarks, stickers, buttons, and certificates encourage enthusiasm for the program. Student-oriented activities accompany each book, and a teacher's guide offers numerous suggestions and ideas for building interest in children's literature. Two sample pages from the OMAR *Teacher's Guide* and *Idea Book* are presented in figures 2.5 and 2.6.[1] The first serves as a discussion guide for the teacher; the second, as an activity page for students.

Figure 2.5
Discussion Guide from the OMAR *Teacher's Guide*

THERE ARE ROCKS IN MY SOCKS ! SAID THE OX TO THE FOX

Division I

AUTHOR: Patricia Thomas

PUBLISHER: Lothrop, Lee and Shepard Company

COPYRIGHT: 1979

SYNOPSIS: An ox has rocks in his socks and cannot figure out a way to get them out. He follows the advice of his friend and the fox ends up in a worse predicament. Finally, a bird comes along and tells the ox how to get rid of the rocks.

AUTHOR'S ADDRESS:

                 c/o Lothrop, Lee and Shepard Company
                 105 Madison Avenue
                 New York, New York 10016

OTHER BOOKS BY THE AUTHOR:

                 "Stand Back," Said the Elephant, "I'm Going to Sneeze!", 1971

BOOK NOTES: 1. The children can write and illustrate rhymes similar to those in the story. (Examples: "I have a pail on my tail," said the quail. "There's a pie in my eye," said the fly.)
                 2. Make a class rock collection or have children make individual collections. These can be displayed and shared with other classes.
                 3. Have the children bring in an old sock to make a hand puppet. Yarn, buttons, rick-rack, and scrap material can be used for decorations.
                 4. After discussing the black and white illustrations in the book, have the children use white paper and black fine-line markers to make their own pictures.

TEACHER'S NOTES:

---

[1]Reprinted by permission of the OMAR Project.

Figure 2.6
Activity Page from the OMAR *Idea Book* for Children

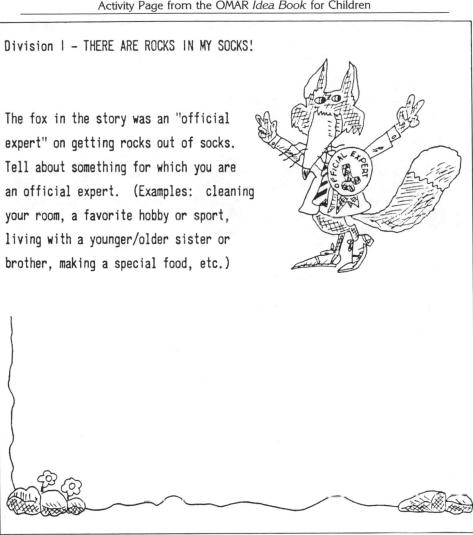

Division I — THERE ARE ROCKS IN MY SOCKS!

The fox in the story was an "official expert" on getting rocks out of socks. Tell about something for which you are an official expert. (Examples: cleaning your room, a favorite hobby or sport, living with a younger/older sister or brother, making a special food, etc.)

REFERENCES

Kranz, Leif and Uif Löfgren. *Children in Water.* Chicago: Children's Press, 1967.

Norton, Donna E. "A Web of Interest." *Language Arts* 54 (November/December 1977): 928–32.

Platt, Penny. "Grapho–Linguistics: Children's Drawings in Relation to Reading and Writing." *The Reading Teacher* 31, no. 3 (December 1977): 262–68.

Sendak, Maurice. *Where the Wild Things Are.* New York: Harper & Row, 1963.

SUGGESTED READINGS

Applebee, Arthur N. "Writing and Reading." *Journal of Reading* 20, no. 6 (March 1977): 534–37.

Arbuthnot, May Hill and Zena Sutherland. *Children and Books*. 4th Ed. Chicago: Scott, Foresman, 1972.

Chomsky, Carol. "Stages in Language Development and Reading Exposure." *Harvard Educational Review* 42 (February 1972): 1–33.

Chomsky, Carol. "Write First, Read Later." *Childhood Education* 47 (March 1971): 296–97.

D'Angelo, Karen, Susan Korba, and Christine Woodworth. "Bookmaking: Motivation for Writing." *Language Arts* 58, no. 3 (March 1981): 308–15.

Gans, Roma. *Guiding Children's Reading Through Experiences*. New York: Teachers College Press, 1979, p. 124.

Gordon, Thomas. *Teacher Effectiveness Training*. New York: Peter H. Wyden, 1974.

Holbrook, Hilary T. "Motivating Reluctant Readers: A Gentle Push." *Language Arts* 59, no. 4 (April 1982): 385–89.

Huck, Charlotte S. and Dorothy Y. Kuhn. *Children's Literature in the Elementary School*. New York: Holt, Rinehart and Winston, 1968.

Norton, Donna E. "A Web of Interest." *Language Arts* 54 (November/December 1977): 928–32.

Smith, Sharon. *Young Authors in the Indianapolis Public Schools: Teachers' Guidebook for Creative Writing and Bookmaking*. Indianapolis: Indianapolis Public Schools, 1977.

Stauffer, Russell G. *The Language Experience Approach to the Teaching of Reading*. New York: Harper and Row, 1970.

Wilson, Marilyn J. "A Review of Recent Research on the Integration of Reading and Writing." *The Reading Teacher* 34, no. 8 (May 1981): 891–901.

Chapter 3

LEARNING TO LISTEN

One of the most frequent complaints in elementary classrooms today is that children just are not listening. Some experts claim that children have been conditioned to a kind of tune-in, tune-out listening by their television watching; others suggest that our noise-filled society fosters poor listening. Whatever the cause, it is certain that listening will have to command an important part in our program of language instruction.

THE ACT OF LISTENING

Listening requires more than the simple reception of sound physiologically. It requires some level of focused perception on the part of the listener in order to selectively discriminate between talk and noise, and between desired messages and other conversations occurring simultaneously. In short, the listener must concentrate attention selectively in order to understand the message being transmitted.

Listening also involves assigning meaning and remembering information from listening. Learners interpret the information they hear and categorize it according to their already existing knowledge. They store this information in memory, perhaps thinking of a purpose for remembering it. In fact, the quality of these thinking and retrieving processes makes the difference between effective and ineffective listening. While we often think of listening as a passive activity, it can be seen that the listener is actively involved in *receiving, attending, understanding,* and *remembering.*

Receiving: Can Students Hear?

Some students simply do not hear the sounds presented to them. Their problem is a physiological one, perhaps involving a degree of hearing impairment. Fortunately, routine tests by school nurses or family physicians can verify the presence or absence of hearing problems so that appropriate classroom measures can be taken.

Attending: Do Students Pay Attention?

Most students with poor listening habits have little experience focusing their attention. They attend globally to all the sounds and stimuli in the classroom at once and are only half tuned-in to classroom instruction. Perhaps the first step in improving listening for these students is to talk about what listening actually involves. Write these two captions on the board: How Not to Listen and How to Listen Successfully. Then ask students to think about their own experiences as listeners and suggest items that could be included under each category. Students may have a surprising range of knowledge to contribute if they are given time to reflect a bit. Their final lists might look like this:

How Not to Listen

Daydream or think about something else.
Think of a song, especially the drum part.
Explore the inside of your desk.
Make small noises with your book or pencil.

How to Listen Successfully

Clear your mind of everything else.
Set a purpose for listening.
Concentrate.
Think about the information, rehearse it.

Listening in a focused way means concentrating one's attention on the incoming message while blocking out other extraneous thoughts and sounds. Students will need to experiment with this kind of attentive listening in order to understand how to do it. The teacher can begin by planning simple focused listening exercises at the beginning of each language arts period. Any of the following activities, which ask for five minutes of focused listening, would be appropriate:

Purpose for Listening	Listening Activity
Predict.	Listen to the opening of a story and predict what might happen next or what might happen in the story as a whole.
Sense mood.	Listen to the beginning of a story and discuss how it makes you feel.
Construct mental images.	Listen to a portion of a story where an interesting character is described and imagine that character.
Trace the story line.	Listen to a short story and retell its events.
Find inconsistencies.	Listen to a mini-mystery and analyze its facts in order to solve it.

These lessons need to show students that they get more information when they really listen. There also need to be times when students think about what they do in order to listen well. Discussions can emphasize that listening involves tuning-in, concentrating, and thinking.

Understanding: Do Students Think as They Listen?

An essential part of effective listening is understanding the incoming information. Students can improve in this area by consciously thinking about their purpose for listening. They can ask, What am I supposed to do with this? or more simply, What is this for?

Students can interpret information from listening by trying to put it in their own words. As they actively listen, they can consider what else they know about the topic and what it suggests to them. Some students may be helped by thinking in terms of categories. They can cluster similar information and relate it to things they already know. Teachers can help by discussing information students have gathered after listening. Questions such as, What other information does this make you think of? and How is this different from what you expected? are helpful in getting students to understand what they have heard.

Remembering: Can Students Remember What They Hear?

One of the first steps in remembering information from listening is to rehearse it. Students can silently say information to themselves, review it, and restate it in their own words. They may also associate information with something that will help them remember it.

The point in this type of listening instruction is that children learn that listening takes some effort. The listener must make a conscious effort to understand and remember information as he listens.

▶ **ideas for student discussion and interaction**

In groups of three, have students play the game How Did It Happen? The purpose of the game is to have students listen to each other and see how much information they can remember. There are three roles to play: the storyteller, the listener, and the judge. The person who is storyteller begins by completing a situation card and making up a story about that situation. The storyteller tells it to the other two members of the group who listen carefully. Then the listener tells the story back, trying to include all the information that can be remembered. The third student, serving as judge, listens to the new version of the story and makes sure that nothing has been forgotten. If anything is missing the judge has to tell what it is.

The teacher's role in this game is twofold. She needs to prepare the situation cards so that they fit the range of experiences
for the class, and she works with each group discussing their experiences as they listen to each other.

The situation cards can suggest childhood adventures or mis-
haps. The following examples may hint at appropriate situations.

> *Situation Cards*
>
> There isn't any change left over from going to the store
>   because . . .
> You lost your jacket (or keys, wallet, sister, bike) when . . .
> The large black spot on the rug was caused by . . .
> Suddenly a soft scraping noise could be heard.
>   It was getting . . .

▶ suggested activities

AS QUIET AS . . . .   A listening experience using music can
stimulate both reflective listening and creative thought. Michael
Colgrass's composition "As Quiet as: A Leaf Turning Colors"
(1968) depicts musically a number of noiseless events. These include a baby sleeping, a mother's smile, and a quiet night. Let
the students listen to this recording and think of other quiet experiences. They may illustrate ideas such as these, which were
suggested by fourth graders:

> *As Quiet as . . .*
>
> a piece of string
> a shadow
> a twinkling star
> a robber creeping

ECHO.   After seeing a film or television program, have students discuss it by playing Echo. This discussion activity involves
two special rules. First, each speaker must echo (tell in a few
words) what the previous speaker said before being allowed to
make his or her own new statement. This rule requires careful
listening. Second, players must always say something new when
they make their statements. This rule requires that students remember what others have said. Everyone in the group must take

a turn (echo the previous statement and make a new statement) and may do so in any order.

LISTENING EXPERIENCES THAT STIMULATE WRITING

(Listening and writing are linked together) in activities occurring almost daily in children's lives. Children listen and write telephone messages routinely and make lists for trips to the grocery store with barely a notice that they are writing.

In the classroom, listening activities have an equally natural link with writing. Listening experiences are commonly used to stimulate student writing. For instance, a teacher may read a story and ask students to write a reaction to it. Teachers often initiate writing by discussing a picture and talking about the mood it presents or the items that are included. These prewriting listening experiences provide young writers with ideas and often with some of the words they will use in writing independently. As activities, they also provide good opportunities to improve the quality of listening that students do.

Each of the writing tasks that follows serves this double purpose; it gives students an opportunity to listen carefully and, by listening, it provides the background needed for students to write independently.

Listening Experience	Writing Task
For five minutes, listen to the sounds of the classroom or the playground.	Write a few sentences describing the sounds that are heard.
Listen as the teacher reads an article from the newspaper.	Write a sentence or two telling a student's opinion about it.
Look at a picture of an interesting place and imagine being there. Discuss what it might be like to be in that particular place.	Write a few sentences describing what it is like to be in the place suggested by the picture.
Listen as a mini-mystery is read aloud.	List the important clues.

Listening Experience	*Writing Task*
Listen to a piece of music. Think about the sounds and the images that are suggested.	Write about an image or idea that the music suggests.
Listen as the first three-fourths of a story are read.	Write a sentence or two predicting how the story will end.
Discuss an emotion (fear, happiness, anger) by telling all the words that it suggests. Example, Fear: scared, scream, dark, cry, run, worry, shadows.	Write a story about something that makes you feel afraid.

Dictation

Another activity that links listening and writing is dictation. The teacher can dictate interesting passages to students using the following procedure. First, read the passage as a whole to acquaint students with its overall meaning. Second, write difficult vocabulary included in the passage on the chalkboard, pronouncing each word as it is written. Third, read the passage in phrases as students write.

Dictation of this sort provides an opportunity for intensive listening and is particularly useful when the teacher does *not* repeat words or go back over sentences. The object of the lessons is for students to see how much of the dictated selection they can get. Students can compete with themselves by trying to get more of the dictated selection each time they have such a lesson.

The passages used for dictation lessons can be riddles or thought problems initially. Later, they can be statements that summarize a concept or provide essential information for content area lessons. The point is that dictation exercises can provide opportunities to extend students' attention span as listeners and also provide practice in listening intently and writing. If word-for-word dictation appears too restrictive, students may opt to write only the main words and then summarize the whole passage in two or three sentences after they finish listening.

▶ **ideas for student discussion and interaction**

(A classroom activity placing students in the role of reporters is ideal for uniting listening and writing skills in an ongoing project. Establish one bulletin board or large display area of the classroom as The Front Page (or whatever your students want to call their classroom newspaper). Teach students to ask questions as reporters do and have them write stories using the information they gather. The articles are then displayed so that the whole center functions as a newspaper front page with everyone's articles available for reading.

A classroom "press conference" can be used to provide training for student reporters. Begin by telling students that reporters use the words *who, what, when, where, why,* and *how* to start their questions. The students can observe reporters in action by watching the nightly television news and noticing the way reporters question whoever is making the news.

Construct the classroom press conference so that there is a real story to write. The teacher can take the role of a person involved in a recent news item with which the class is familiar. Students will need to know whom they are interviewing, what the situation is, and what some of the details are. Once the situation is established, give children time to write their questions. Conduct a ten-minute news conference letting students ask their questions and instructing them to listen to all the information that is given. At the end of the press conference all the reporters are to write their stories using their notes and the information they remember from listening. The news stories get posted on The Front Page as the first offerings.

The newspaper project can be expanded by planning particular features or topics for various columns. Students can consider whether there should be a sports column, a place for school news, and a section for national news. Reporters can write articles and post their final copies in appropriate columns, making The Front Page a constantly changing display.

▶ **suggested activities**

WHO IS IT?   In the format of a riddle, have students write a description of someone who is familiar to everyone in the class.

The "mystery person" could be a character from a television program or book, or it could be a person in the classroom itself. The description needs to mention the characteristics that distinguish that person from others and must include what the person is known for, where he can be found, and what he or she looks like. The "Who Is It?" descriptions can be used as listening lessons for the class. The author reads the riddle and answers questions that students pose. Students hearing the riddle try to guess the identity by asking for more information, listening to the answers they get, jotting down pieces of information, and writing their answers to the riddle.

TELEPHONE MESSAGES.   For this listening and writing activity, have students work in pairs to simulate the kind of telephone messages they commonly take. Both students can begin by constructing a situation in which four or five bits of information are to be given as a telephone message. The students then take turns listening to and writing the messages they hear from their partner. The goal of these simulations is for the listener to understand the message accurately and write a message that clearly represents the information.

FAIRY TALE RADIO SHOWS.   The purpose of this activity is to change a piece of literature from one form to another—from a narrative story to a play—and to incorporate the newly created play into a particular kind of listening experience, a radio show.

Let students listen to recordings of old radio shows and their commercials and then discuss what these programs did to create excitement and capture interest.[1] Discuss how sound effects, music, and voice inflections made the broadcasts seem real.

Begin the writing experience by dividing students into small groups with each group choosing a particular fairy tale to dramatize. Students must read the fairy tale and become familiar with its major characters and events. They may even want to look for other versions of the same fairy tale and choose among possible plot variations. Encourage students to talk their way through the plot and jot down major events to include in their play. Then

---

[1]For tapes of old radio shows, write Cassette Library, P.O. Box 5331, Baltimore, MD 21209.

have students write the play and test out various sections by reading them aloud, listening for excitement and effectiveness.

Once the fairy tale scripts are complete, children can create a radio show using the fairy tale as its central feature. The show may contain an introduction, the fairy tale play, commercials, sound effects, and even music. These radio shows can be recorded and placed in classroom listening centers or they can be shared with other classes. Particularly exciting shows could even be aired over the school P.A. system or broadcast for the public from a radio station.

PERSONAL MYTHS AND LEGENDS.   Myths and legends are particularly interesting kinds of literature to read aloud and can be used to stimulate original student writing. To begin this listening/writing activity, find myths or legends related to whatever is currently being studied in the classroom and have students listen as they are read aloud. Discuss the similarities among the myths and legends so students can identify the common characteristics. Encourage students to write their own myths or legends on subjects of personal interest. Some sample topics might be: legends about sharks or other animals, myths about why flowers have different colors (create a flower goddess), myths about hurricanes (create a hurricane god), or myths about cavities (create a cavity god).

The writings may be enclosed in a book with illustrations and placed in the classroom or school library. Students could also visit other classrooms and read their myths and legends aloud during story time.

TEACHING STUDENTS TO LISTEN TO DIRECTIONS

It is disconcerting to realize that even though students may hear directions, they may not be listening to them. Listening to directions requires that students prepare for action. Their role is to translate what they hear (the directions) into meaning (a particular set of actions). Perhaps what goes wrong with direction-giving in classrooms is that students do not listen with this special purpose in mind. In fact, our observations in classrooms reveal that students listen to directions rather passively. It is interesting to note that when the directions are over, these passive listeners commonly take on a surprised appearance. They are unaware that they are supposed to "do something." Two patterns of action follow: first, they request a rerun (Would you repeat the directions?); second, they ask a neighbor (What are we supposed to do?).

The way around this dilemma is to teach students to listen to directions purposefully. They must *be prepared to do something* after hearing directions. This purposeful listening raises the expectation of having to follow through or act on the information gathered through listening. It also necessitates a special level of attention. Students concentrate on the directions, attending to their general intent and their specific information.

In summary, listening to directions involves:

1. Listening purposefully (finding out what to do)
2. Attending to both general information and specific instructions

▶ **ideas for student discussion and interaction**

Have students discuss how they listen to directions. The following questions may be used to stimulate the students to evaluate their listening habits.

- What is the difference between listening to directions and other kinds of listening, such as listening to a story or listening to an oral report? (If there are no ideas, try both kinds of listening and have students describe the differences.)
- What does a person who is a good listener do when listening to directions?
- What personal strategies do you use to successfully listen during direction-giving?
- What problems occur when you are listening to directions?
- Are the directions given orally in one subject more difficult than those given in another?
- What solutions can be suggested for dealing with difficulties encountered when following directions in difficult subjects?
- What advice do you have for students who want to do a better job of this kind of listening?

At the end of the discussion have students summarize orally their approach to listening when directions are being given. The teacher may write this summary on the board for students to use before the next listening experience involving directions.

Once students are aware that listening to directions requires special attention and purposefulness, a number of activities can be used to help students improve.

▶ **suggested activities**

FOLLOW THE TRAIL.   Give students a sheet of graph paper with large squares and have them place at fixed locations key landmarks in their neighborhood. The grid will serve as a crude map that locates school, home, shopping centers, key streets, parks, friends' houses, creeks, and even bike trails. The first training in listening to directions is to listen as the teacher directs students to number the lines on the grid so that reference points are established. For instance, the map in figure 3.1 has all the horizontal lines numbered evenly and all of the vertical ones labeled with odd numbers. The teacher then gives directions on where to position all the major landmarks to appear on the map. For example, the teacher might say, "Insert the school at the crossing point of lines number 3 and 4. Draw Jamison Park in the top right-hand corner, bounded by lines 11 and 2, and show the bike path that runs around its edge." The point of this lesson, as the oral directions continue, is that careful listening to directions is essential in order for an accurate map to be drawn. At the end of the lesson, students compare their map with the original and adjust any locations that are incorrect.

Once the maps are standardized, tape a piece of plastic over the top of each one so that the students can mark a trail they hear described in a listening game. Before play begins, students must write stories, fictional or true, that tell about their adventures in the neighborhood. Story starters such as these will be helpful:

A typical afternoon after school takes me from . . .
The best way to get to Jamison Park is . . .

Students play Follow the Trail by listening in small groups as one class member reads his story. The others mark with crayon

Figure 3.1
Sample "Follow the Trail" Map

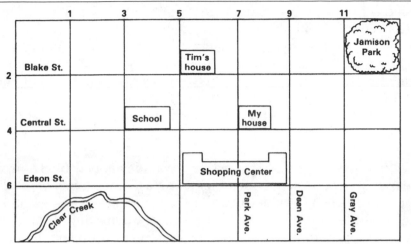

or washable marker the trail that is described in the story. At the end, the reader checks each trail for accuracy and chooses the next reader from among the students who successfully followed the story trail. Each map can be wiped clean of the previous trail marks in preparation for the new story.

ORIGAMI PROJECTS.   Simple origami projects provide another activity for teaching students to attend to oral directions. Origami, the traditional Oriental paper-folding craft, involves making simple objects such as boats, birds, or flowers from brightly colored paper that has been folded in particular patterns.

To use origami with small groups of children, develop three or four projects that involve simple directions. Write a set of directions for each project or get a set from a book of origami activities. Have a student read the directions to the other group members, who follow them step by step. The origami project serves as a listening lesson for receiving step-by-step directions. After the projects are completed, discuss how students went about following the directions and what hints they learned for successful listening.

SHADOW PLAYS.   Students often like to make hand shadows in particular forms (such as ducks quacking or birds flying) in the bright light from a movie projector or a flashlight. Let students who find these shadow patterns interesting develop written directions for making particularly interesting shadows. Test out the effectiveness of both the written directions and the students' ability to follow them by having a shadow play demonstration in front of the class. The author of the directions may read the directions orally while a volunteer places his hands in the beam of light and attempts to make the desired form. The class may evaluate the quality of both the directions and the direction-following that they observe.

ZERO VISIBILITY.   This activity was developed by Thomas Devine in his excellent book of listening activities, *Listening Skills Schoolwide* (1982). Devine suggests that students play a game in which students "talk down" an airplane attempting to land in conditions of zero visibility. The class selects a controller who provides the directions and a pilot who is blindfolded. Using the directions provided by the controller, the pilot must land the plane on the runway and avoid the obstacles (desks, chairs, tables) that have been placed in the way.

CHALKBOARD ANIMALS.   Students are given practice following oral directions at the chalkboard when they participate in this activity. Have students listen as step-by-step directions are given for drawing an animal. The directions must indicate what shapes to draw and what forms to connect. The listener's purpose is to listen and follow the directions accurately, producing the desired animal. Oral directions can be given with more than one instruction at a time so that students can practice listening to directions carefully.

Additional listening activities for following directions are included in chapter 8.

TEACHING STUDENTS TO LISTEN CRITICALLY

Critical listening involves thinking carefully during the act of listening. It invites the listener to adopt a skeptical perspective, scrutinizing the language and the information in the message

being received. The following humorous quotation captu
special perspective and its attending difficulties.

> I know you believe you understood
> what you think I said, but I am
> not sure you realize that what
> you heard is not what I meant. (Lundsteen, 1979, p. 21)

Analyzing Language as Emotional or Neutral

As students listen, they can analyze the kinds of language they are hearing and ask themselves whether the words are emotional or neutral. Emotional words stimulate an emotional reaction or appeal primarily to feeling, while neutral words convey meaning without the overlay of emotion.

Students can gain awareness of this distinction by listening as their teacher reads a newspaper article and emphasizes words that are interesting choices. A second reading of these words after the article itself has been read can help students consider each word's emotional impact and help them categorize the words as either emotional or neutral. Students may then discuss their list of emotional words and give reasons for their categorizations.

Once students realize that writers of news items, commercials, and political speeches often choose words on the basis of their emotional content, they can begin listening critically and noticing when emotional words are used and why.

Television commercials are good subjects for analysis. Have the students listen and try to capture the general emotion that the commercials suggest, noticing the particular words that convey the desired message. Have the students write down some examples they hear during their home listening, and discuss them as a class.

Listening for Completeness

As students grow in their ability to listen critically, they may begin to look for completeness in their listening experiences. Many speeches or statements of opinion leave out vital information that is crucial to understanding. This missing information usually has an adverse effect on the particular argument the speaker is making.

That, of course, is generally the reason for leaving it out.

Students, as critical listeners, need to listen to political speeches with questions in mind, such as, What other information is there on this issue? or What is the speaker leaving out that is important?

Students can listen for examples of incomplete information as they watch political figures make statements to the press on television newscasts. During class discussions, students can share examples of incomplete information they have gathered and also discuss what the missing information was and why it was left out.

Considering the Credentials of the Speaker

Another aspect of critical listening is considering the credentials of the speaker. Children can ask whether the speaker is an authority on the subject he is talking about or whether his area of expertise or importance comes from a different area. Students can consider, for example, the most important issues of the day and then identify who has the best credentials to provide comment and information about them. A list of such issues and authorities might include:

Issue	Authority
nuclear arms negotiations	chief U.S. negotiator
state of the economy	Secretary of the Treasury
farm conditions	Secretary of Agriculture
safety of the city bridges	city engineer
quality of the local schools	school board member

Students may also suggest speakers for each issue who would not be acceptable. For instance, a cab driver would not have the credentials to be considered an authority on farm conditions or the state of the economy. The cabbie might be an expert on a certain city bridge, having driven over it and watched its girders rust for twenty years. Even with this firsthand experience, information from an expert on bridges would be desirable and necessary.

Once students have seen how to evaluate appropriate authorities for a given topic, they can listen critically as public figures comment on issues of the day and sports figures recommend various kinds of cereal, sports cars, and shaving cream. Students may want to collect examples of appropriate and inappropriate experts giving their opinions. Students should consider the qualifications of the speaker as an important aspect in determining the value of the speaker's opinions.

Listening for Fact and Opinion

Critical listening implies that the receiver of a message has some standards against which to make judgments of worth or believability. One standard that elementary school students can use is the proportion of fact to opinion. If a listening experience consists primarily of opinion, it is less credible than one based primarily on fact.

As students listen to media broadcasts or conversations they can ask themselves, Is this information factual (can I verify or check it out?) or is it an opinion (an expression of an individual's feelings or reactions to a given subject)? While it would be erroneous to value only facts and discount opinion, it certainly is true that listening critically involves working from a basic understanding of the facts.

Students may build an understanding of this distinction by participating in the following listening activity. Select pairs of Letters to the Editor from the local paper that present conflicting opinions about an important issue familiar to students. Read the letters to the students asking them to compare the facts that each of the two sides use (are any left out by one side or the other?) and consider the basis for the opinions that are stated. Ask students then to make a critical judgment about which is the most sensible letter on the basis of this comparison. Have students support their judgments with verifiable information.

Critical listening involves an awareness of not only the credibility of information, but also the appropriateness of the language it is couched in and the completeness of the information presented.

Activities involving critical thinking are also included in chapter 7.

REFERENCES

Colgrass, Michael. "As Quiet as: A Leaf Turning Colors," RCA Victor LSC-3001, Boston Symphony Orchestra, 1968.

Devine, Thomas G. *Listening Skills Schoolwide*. Urbana, Ill.: ERIC Clearinghouse on Reading and Communication Skills, National Institute of Education, National Council of Teachers of English, 1982.

Lundsteen, Sara W. *Listening: Its Impact on Reading and the Other Language Arts*. Urbana, Ill.: ERIC Clearinghouse on Reading and Communication Skills, National Institute of Education, National Council of Teachers of English, 1979.

SUGGESTED READINGS

Devine, Thomas G. "Listening: What Do We Know After Fifty Years of Research and Theorizing?" *Journal of Reading* 21, no. 4 (1978): 269–74.

Devine, Thomas G. *Listening Skills Schoolwide*. Urbana, Ill.: ERIC Clearinghouse on Reading and Communication Skills, National Institute of Education, National Council of Teachers of English, 1982.

Lundsteen, Sara W. *Children Learn to Communicate*. Englewood Cliffs, N.J.: Prentice-Hall, 1976.

Lundsteen, Sara W. *Listening: Its Impact on Reading and Other Language Arts*. Urbana, Ill.: ERIC Clearinghouse on Reading and Communication Skills, National Institute of Education, National Council of Teachers of English, 1979.

Pearson, P. David and Linda Fielding. "Listening, Comprehension." *Language Arts* 59, no. 6 (September 1982): 617–27.

Tutolo, Daniel. "Critical Listening/Reading Advertisements." *Language Arts* 58, no. 6 (September 1981): 679–83.

Wright, Jone Perryman and Lester Laminack. "First Graders Can Be Critical Listeners and Readers." *Language Arts*. 59, no. 2 (February 1982): 133–36.

Chapter 4

PROBLEMS WITH WORDS: PHONICS AND SPELLING

Even though pronouncing words while reading is different from spelling them accurately while writing, there are similar features to teaching those skills. The basic similarity is that the sound-spelling patterns of the English language are intimately involved in both pronunciation and spelling.

In reading, the learner sees the word in print (in context) and tries to relate the word to one that already exists in his head or in his hearing vocabulary. Since getting the meaning of the message is the primary preoccupation, the reader uses only those cues sufficient to satisfy him that he has achieved the meaning of the sentence—and that may mean pronouncing an unfamiliar word. Details within a word are not considered important to the reader; the emphasis is on recognizing the word as familiar or not, or in getting the word's meaning from context if it is a word outside his vocabulary.

In writing or spelling, on the other hand, the writer already has the word he wants to use in his head. What he needs are accurate symbols to transcribe those words to someone else. To accomplish that feat requires considerable attention to the details of English spelling. It is not sufficient, as with reading, to use minimal cues. Now the job is to employ a specific knowledge of English sound-spelling patterns and a concentrated visual memory of printed words in order to deliver a written message that other people can read.

(Reading and writing are reinforcing activities, there is no doubt about that. The more one reads, the more likely he or she will feel comfortable with the spelling task in writing. The reader's visual memory is ready to know whether or not a word "looks right" when written down. As the writer pays closer attention to words, spelling patterns, and structural parts while writing, he is sharpening his insight into the system that will help him pronounce words that he does not at first recognize when reading.)

In this chapter we discuss a strategy for word recognition and phonics and a strategy for spelling. The commonality of the strategies rests in the assumption that children are (pattern-seeking learners who will improve in reading and in writing (spelling) as they see that the English spelling system is manageable.) They realize they can gain control over it as they learn across the years.

In the back of this book are four appendices that classroom teachers may find useful in developing phonics and spelling activities. These appendices include a list of common Latin and Greek roots and prefixes, a list of frequent vowel and consonant combinations, a list of English sound-spelling generalizations, and common phonics terms.

A STRATEGY FOR UNKNOWN WORDS

We want children to gain a sense of power over words from the outset of reading instruction. Not only should they get an early sense of how to read a message, but they should know that they can solve the English spelling system, that the system is regular, and that they can learn the rules gradually.

The following strategy for teaching decoding in reading encourages the reader to be efficient, that is, to use the smallest possible number of cues in identifying unknown words. In combination with using the context of the word, the reader is taught to utilize the decoding technique or strategy in a rapid series of decisions such as the following:

1. Using context and the beginning of the word, can I determine its pronunciation? For example: I dove into the water in search of *tr*(easure).

2. Using No. 1 plus a common (graphemic) base (-sure), can I determine its pronunciation?
3. Using No. 2 plus known phonics generalizations, can I determine pronunciation?
4. If I still cannot figure it out, should I look up the word or ask someone to help me?

By systematically and daily approaching unknown words in that way, the teacher teaches the children a way of thinking about words. In the sentence, "He dove into the water in search of _____," the reader has numerous, legitimate hypothesized words that fit the blank. The word must be a noun or a pronoun. It will be something that can be found beneath the water. Depending on additional information or context, the hypothesis could be more specific, for example, a species of fish. If the sentence stood all by itself, the options are numerous: fish, sunken ships, treasure, coral, caves, and so on.

If context and use of a sound-symbol correspondence at the beginning of the word offer enough clues to make the word click in the reader's mind, no further analysis is necessary. If not, the next step is to search for familiar patterns. In the early reading stages, children have few patterns to search for. As their knowledge of patterns of written letters representing spoken sounds (graphemic bases) expands and as they practice reading more and more, the number of accessible graphemic bases increases, and they can be used more automatically.

Where no familiar pattern of consonants and vowels can be identified, the child then works through the letters, trying to apply whatever phonics generalizations are available. If context and decoding (phonics) clues do not produce a recognizable word, the child can ask for help or go to the dictionary.

GRAPHEMIC BASE TECHNIQUE

Since the speaker of English does not hear isolated letter sounds, but rather tends to hear sounds clumped together in words or syllables, an effective phonics (decoding) technique will take advantage of that circumstance. In searching for order in words, the ear and eye sort things by similarities and differences, especially differences (Fries, 1962). In other words, the listener and reader of English work out the sound-spelling system by paying attention to contrasts. A listener knows the difference between the sounds of *pan* and *fan* by separating the part that sounds the same from the part that is different. He does not sort out *p-a-n* to see how those three elements sound different from *f-a-n*. His ear notes that *-an* is the same, and *p-* and *f-* are different. In a sentence, the context may give a cue to trigger the appropriate contrastive feature. Context does not help in a sentence such as: Go to the store and buy a _an. The listener (or reader) has to distinguish the word by recognizing the specific consonant sound *p-* or *f-*.

To apply that concept to reading leads to a decoding or phonics technique called a graphemic base technique. To understand the technique, think of word families or rhyming words—for example, the *-ad* group:

bad	b-ad	I feel bad.
dad	d-ad	Dad loves me.
fad	f-ad	Jeans are a fad.
had	h-ad	I had a dog.
cad	c-ad	What a cad!
lad	l-ad	He's a nice lad.
mad	m-ad	I am mad.
pad	p-ad	That's my pad of paper.

Put a few examples on the board and ask the children to see how many words they can add to the list, but they must be able to use the word in a sentence. Use simple patterns for beginners:

b-id	b-it	b-et	c-ot
d-id	f-it	g-et	h-ot

Use more difficult patterns for more experienced readers:

h-igh	s-igh

Graphemic Bases

The following is a list of graphemic bases that can lead to many words and sentences:

-able	-am	-eer	-ig	-ment	-ow
-ack	-ash	-ence	-igh	-ob	-oy
-ad	-at	-end	-ill	-ook	-sion
-ail	-ation	-ent	-im	-ong	-ture
-ain	-awk	-et	-ind	-op	-ug
-air	-ay	-ible	-ip	-ot	-ump
-all	-ear	-ick	-it	-ound	-un
-and	-ed	-ied	-ition	-ous	-ut

By relying on known, common grouped sounds such as *-ad* or *-an* or *-ic* as a base, a teacher can show a learner how to build words or distinguish words in the *-ad* group by changing the initial sound-letter. The *-ad* becomes a graphemic base, a consistent sound-spelling pattern on which to build. By using simple three-letter words (trigraphs such as *bad*, *had*) to begin the decoding process, children will gradually build their repertoire of graphemic bases and increase their sense of independence in solving word problems.

PHONICS TECHNIQUE

Phonics Associations

Phonics is translating parts of written words into the sounds they represent. For example, the beginning reader learns the sound of *th* in *thick*. This gives him a clue to the pronunciation of other words like *thing*, *third*, and *thank*. He learns the sound of *ck* in *back*, which gives him a clue to the sound he sees in *clock*, *truck*, *stick*, and *check*. Thus, each time a phonics element is introduced or discussed, ask children to think of other words that have the same sound. List on the chalkboard those words that exhibit the element under discussion. Children thereby learn to look for known letters that stand for the same speech sound or sounds.

Phonograms

Letters that stand for speech sounds are called phonograms. The letters *scr* in *scream*, *t* in *cat*, *aw* in *saw*, and *oa* in *boat* are phonograms. A phonogram is a letter or a group of letters that stands for a speech sound. The letter *t* in *cat* stands for a single speech sound. *Scr* in *scream* stands for a blending of sounds. *Sat* in *satisfy* stands for a syllable. Every syllable phonogram has a single vowel (cat) or it may be two or more vowels pronounced as one sound (eat). See Appendix B, "Frequent Phonograms: Vowels and Consonants" for additional examples.

▶ **suggested activities**

PHONOGRAM PACK.   This game feeds off the current game craze, and the aim is to produce more words than your opponent. Form teams of three or four students. Two teams are pitted against each other in trying to outdo each other in producing words that contain certain phonograms. The teacher provides the phonograms that may be used in the game—usually three or four—and the starting team may produce a word that fits any of the identified phonograms, for example, *scr* in *scream*, *aw* in *saw*, and *oa* in *boat*. The two teams continue to produce words alternately for one phonogram until a team cannot think of another word. The team to say the last correct word wins that round and may then initiate the next phonogram for round two. Many of these competing teams may operate in the classroom at the same time.

PHONICS AT HOME.   Send home suggestions for practice exercises that parents can do with their young children. Preschool children should have plenty of opportunity to listen to clear speech and to imitate it. This is excellent preparation for phonics skill-building later on.

When children play with alphabet blocks, they may ask about the letters. Parents should answer those questions. It paves the way for phonics learning. A parent need not try to teach all the letter names, or try to teach alphabetical order. Forced learning may create an unfavorable attitude toward reading. The child will learn those skills best when he or she actually needs to use them later on.

Children sometimes ask about a word they see. Telling them what the word is helps them relate printed language to spoken language.

Children often like to play with the sounds of words. Listening to rhymes and jingles helps them build a foundation for phonics. So does making up rhymes and repeating sounds that they like.

Children also like being read to. Listening to books sharpens awareness of and appreciation for the sounds of spoken language. It leads children to experiment with words and it helps them build a larger vocabulary.

MAKE YOUR OWN RULE.   Students should be encouraged to construct their own phonics rules. They learn several words with the same beginning consonant (ball, big, boy). Then they may listen to the first consonant sounds of other words beginning with *b*. Ask them to identify the sound that the letter *b* makes in each word.

PATTERN PARTY.   Other phonics programs encourage the student to associate sounds with letter patterns. The student is shown the letter-sound patterns in words, such as a short vowel sound pattern. The words *mad, pet, bit, pop,* and *cut* are typical of the consonant-vowel-consonant pattern with the short vowel sound. The student then learns a long vowel sound pattern. *Made, Pete, bite, rope,* and *cute* are typical of the consonant-vowel-consonant-vowel pattern with a long middle vowel and a so-called silent *e* on the end. Actually the final *e* helps spell the long vowel sound. This sound-spelling pattern method gives the child phonics guidelines from the beginning. After each pattern is introduced, have the students volunteer examples to be listed on the chalkboard. Be sure the students understand the pattern and are not offering only rhyming words.

Beginning Phonograms: Common Consonant Combinations

A beginning reader must learn to look for phonics clues in all parts of a word. These clues can be found at the beginning of the word, in the middle, or at the end.

The following list includes special combinations as well as blends of beginning phonograms. A special combination, like *th* or *sh*, stands for a consonant sound that is distinct from the sound each letter represents alone.

Phonogram	Examples	Phonogram	Examples
st	stay, stop	dr	draw, dress
sh	she, shoe	fr	friend, from
ch (tsh)	chair, child	bl	black, blow
th (voiceless)	thank, thin	pl	place, play
th (voiced)	the, them	fl	flag, flower
cr	crack, crow	sw	sweet, swim
tr	train, tree	pr	present, prize
sp	speak, spin	wr	write, wrong
br	bright, bring	sm	small, smile
gr	grass, green	sn	snake, sneeze
cl	clean, clock	squ (skw)	square, squeak
wh (hw)	what, when	gl	glad, glass
sl	sleep, slide	tw	twelve, twin

Ending Phonograms: Common Consonant Combinations

In learning end sounds, the student listens for a sound like the *n* in *ten*, as the teacher pronounces the word. Then he identifies the same last consonant sound in other spoken words. Finally he identifies the letter that represents that sound as the words are written on the chalkboard. His experience with beginning consonants helps him to identify ending consonants.

After the student has some experience with single ending consonants, he goes on to other word endings. He learns the *-s* and *-es* endings (ducks, boxes, and helps); the *-d* and *-ed* endings (surprised and climbed); and the *-ing* ending (working). He learns the *'s* and *s'* endings (girl's, girls'); the *-er* and *-est* endings (stronger, strongest); and common suffixes such as *-ful* (helpful), *-en* (eaten), *-y* (stormy), *-ly* (really), and *-less* (restless).

The following list contains some common ending phonograms.

Phonogram	Examples	Phonogram	Examples
nd	and, bend	ld	bold, build
ng	among, bring	ch	beach, church
ll	ball, call	th	bath, breath
ck	back, neck	nk	bank, drink
st	best, dust	ft	drift, gift
nt	ant, front	mp	camp, jump
ss	brass, cross	ct	act, expect
sh	dish, fresh		

Vowels and Diphthongs

The reader must also learn to identify the sounds of vowels and diphthongs. There are fifteen common vowel and diphthong sounds, but only seven letters are used to represent them. These letters are *a, e, i, o, u,* and sometimes *y* and *w.* Vowel sounds are represented by a variety of phonograms. For instance, the short sound of *e* is represented most frequently by *e* in *set,* and less frequently by *ai* in *again, ea* in *ready, ie* in *friend, ay* in *says, ue* in *guess,* and *a* in *many.*

Short vowel sounds in single vowel words like *back, next, twin,* and *rock* are easiest to learn, so teachers usually begin with that pattern. After some experience with it, the student works out a personal phonics guideline. He now knows that a single vowel sound at the beginning or in the middle of a one-syllable word often has the short sound. He then applies this guideline to other words, including words of more than one syllable.

The long sounds of *a, i,* and *o* in words like *safe, wife,* and *rode* are fairly easy to learn, so they are usually taught before other long vowel patterns. The student may begin with one such long vowel—as the *a* in *safe, ate, cake,* and *face.* After working with it, the student comes to realize that the *a* is long and the *e* "silent." Long *i* and long *o* are taught in the same pattern, and the student works out another phonics guideline. He now knows that when a one-syllable word ends in a final *e,* the preceding vowel is often long.

Vowel sounds represented by two letters are found in many words. Examples are *ay* in *say, ai* in *nail, ea* in *seat,* and *oa* in *oak.*

Students working with such words soon realize that often the first vowel is long, the second silent. There are always exceptions, of course.

Certain vowel sounds and matching dual letters are called diphthongs. Some diphthongs are taught separately. Students learn the *ou* sound in words such as *south* and *how*; they learn the *oi* sound in words such as *noise* and *boy*.

Children also work with vowel letters followed by *r*. They come to understand that even though the vowel spelling changes, the sound stays much the same. Examples in accented syllables are *ir* in *bird*, *ur* in *turn*, *er* in *her*, *or* in *worse*, *our* in *courtesy*, *urr* in *purr*, *ear* in *early*, *yr* in *myrtle*, and *ere* in *were*. Examples in unaccented syllables are *er* in *father*, *or* in *sailor*, and *ar* in *dollar*.

Using Phonics Skills

Identifying phonograms and blending their sounds help students recognize words, but the final test of phonics skills is how they handle new words. A new word has a new combination of phonograms. The students may know *oa* in *boat*, but do they recognize it in *goat*?

Students usually come across new words every time they read a new story, so they must learn to use phonics and other reading skills so quickly and accurately that the skills become automatic. The purpose of phonics and other word analysis skills is to help students read by themselves.

SOUND-SPELLING PATTERNS

Inventive Spelling

In the English language there are a number of sound-spelling patterns that predict what the spelling will be. Most students in the upper elementary or secondary grades have a sense of that sound-spelling relationship. They may make mistakes, but they have a sense of the phonetic connection and often invent spellings that can be understood because they are "spelled as they sound."

Students should be encouraged to use that sense of inventive spelling in their rough drafts. At the point where they are trying to organize ideas and get them on paper, the message is the critical factor. Accurate spelling becomes a factor when the paper is to be submitted to someone else for reading. As they write words whose spelling is doubtful, they could circle them for checking later. In proofreading the rough draft, students can refer to known sound-spelling generalizations to guide them. (See Appendix C, "Phonics Generalizations.") The following activities can alert students to those patterns.

▶ **suggested activities**

THE RHYME GAME.   Words that rhyme have played a part in everyone's childhood. From nursery rhymes in early childhood to rhyming poems, from jingles in commercials on radio and television to identifying similarities in words that are read—these rhyme forms all contribute to a person's sense of sound-spelling patterns. Rhyme forms vary from the simplest kind, such as *cat*, *rat*, and *bat*, to those that are more complex and use multiple spellings for the same sounds, such as *snow*, *though*, and *hoe*. Rhyme games can be fun and useful as a quick exercise to develop spelling consciousness.

Select words that need attention and ask the class to see how many words with similar sounds they can come up with. At the start the words should be oral and not written on the chalkboard. By writing on the chalkboard, the students may rely on a visual image of the word rather than its sound. The students can call out words that rhyme with the cue word, and then each individual develops his or her own list.

When the class runs out of ideas for words that rhyme with the cue word, the various words can be listed on the chalkboard and can be categorized under appropriate spelling patterns. The final sounds of *snow*, *though*, and *hoe* are indications of patterns that could exist for rhyming words with the final long *o* sound. The following list provides other patterns.

Sample Sound-Spelling Patterns

atch, etch, itch	ission
ackle, ickle	ize
amble, emble, umble	arge, erge, urge

anch, ench, inch, unch	own
ance, ence, ince	able, ible
addle, iddle, uddle	oil
adge, edge, idge, odge, udge	ect, ection
air	ous
ear	ies, ied, ying
ary	ture

By looking at the patterns on the chalkboard, students are asked to develop their own generalizations or senses of how that sound might be spelled. Such guidelines give them alternatives that can be used in spelling common sounds in the future.

Graphemic Bases

Rhyming sounds are those that refer to the vowel and the ending sound in a word, for example the *at* in *cat*, *rat*, and *bat*. Some authorities refer to the similarity of a spelling for a given sound as a recurring graphemic base—that is, the same symbols are used to spell a similar sound. Thus, the *ow* in *snow* is the graphemic base for the *o* sound in *snow*, *glow*, *flow*, *blow*, and so on. Ask children to think of words that contain the targeted sound. As they say them, write them on the board in a list to emphasize the regularity of the graphemic base. If a word with different pattern is mentioned, place it in a separate column, for example:

lie	high
pie	sigh
die	

This rhyme exercise should be brief and quick. It could be done on a daily basis for a while and then periodically to remind students to use it as a way of becoming more conscious of spelling patterns.

Advanced Patterns

The level of sophistication of the learner should dictate what kinds of sound-spelling patterns will be chosen for discussion. For example, students who are having extreme difficulties with spelling should work on spelling patterns that have high frequency and make use of those. The consonant-vowel-consonant pattern (cat, bed, dip, hop, but) represents very frequently occurring patterns that have a high percentage of regularity. Some students may not realize that they can use those patterns in helping themselves spell other words. The so-called silent *e* is actually a marker for the long sound of the vowel in such words as *game*, *Pete*, *bite*, *rode*, and *cute* and is another pattern that can be used by students who have very low-level spelling skills. Those who are more advanced can examine more difficult patterns, even some from other languages:

astrology	bureau	barrette	dynamic
biology	plateau	cigarette	ceramic
chronology	chateau	etiquette	organic
geology	beau	roulette	mechanic
sociology	tableau		satanic

VISUAL SENSE IN SPELLING

Ear-Eye Training

In interviews with many good spellers, we found that they employ hunches in trying to spell difficult words. They hear the word, make a guess at how it should be spelled, and then write it. Once they have written the word, they examine it to see if their eye confirms their hunch. If their eye finds some fault, that is, if their visual memory of the word is upset, then they check the word further by asking someone else or by using the dictionary. Making hunches or hypothesizing about difficult words is helpful because it encourages students to think and act. A student should not stop dead simply because he does not know exactly how to spell a word. While writing, students make the best guess they can. Their ear dictates a kind of spelling that can be checked later during proofreading.

▶ **suggested activities**

EAR-EYE HUNCHES.   Ordinarily those who read extensively have built into their visual memory a sense of how words should look in print. That does not mean that every avid reader is going to be an excellent speller, but it does mean that the visual memory is storing all kinds of images that help in the confirmation process. This should be explained to students as part of the confirmation process. Two "hunch" exercises are presented here to help students strengthen their spelling aptitude.

1. Encourage students to make hunches and to get themselves used to using their eye as a confirming source once a hunch is written. Take a selection from a student's paper and read it aloud, asking students to spell particular words; alternatively, read from a word list, asking the students to make a guess as to how a word is spelled. Then the correct spelling of the word may be written on the board by the teacher or by a student.

2. Have a rough-draft writing exercise and ask students to circle words where they stopped to make hunches. When they have completed the draft, they should go back through and ask their eyes to tell them if there is something wrong. Through checking with the sound-spelling patterns that they know or checking with their neighbors or a dictionary, they should confirm whether the circled words are correct or not.

Misspelled words should be written correctly above the circled word. In a nonthreatening setting the students gain a sense that using hunches is part of the process of learning: sometimes hunches are on target and sometimes they miss the mark. A quick perusal of a paper may also reveal additional words that need correcting. The teacher may want to circle them in colored ink and return the paper for correction. The papers are then resubmitted to show that correction has occurred.

PRACTICE WRITING AND SPELLING

Testing Spelling in Writing

As the old adage goes, practice makes perfect. Research has demonstrated that the more time spent on tasks, the greater the improvement. Thus, the more time spent in writing with a concern for spelling the more likely spelling will improve.

There are certain limitations to the practice-makes-perfect guideline. If a student has no sense of how to improve, the practice activity may in fact confirm bad habits in spelling. Writing practice should help the writer become conscious of her need to communicate and to improve communication. Sharing papers with peers and producing papers for display are the kinds of activities that may motivate a writer to improve in spelling—one aspect of written communication.

▶ **suggested activities**

THE 300-WORD SPELLING TEST.   One way to improve everyday writing is to have children produce a weekly 300-word writing sample to proofread for spelling errors. The point of the exercise is to reduce week-by-week the number of errors in a 300-word sample.

For the purpose of improving spelling, the teacher has the students write a composition of at least 300 words. Three hundred words are then marked off for a spelling check. Sometimes the first 300 words are used; sometimes 300 words are taken from another part of a longer composition.

Errors may be checked by a team correction approach. Each member of the team marks off his 300-word sample and then circulates the sample among the members of a three- to six-member team. Each reads what the other has written and circles suspected spelling errors.

The number found in the 300-word sample is then tallied after all members of the team have read the samples and each person records the number of errors that he made for that day. A simple grid similar to the one shown in figure 4.1 can be used for recording errors from week to week.

Over the period of two months to a semester errors will be reduced. An error reduction chart helps students set goals for improvement. They are competing against themselves.

ALTERNATIVE: TEACHER EVALUATES 300 WORDS.   By having the students write regularly in a notebook or log the teacher can select at random a 300-word sample to be evaluated. The student first does his own review of the 300-word sample by circling the words he thinks are misspelled. The student then shows the sample to the teacher who adds circles or confirms that the student has correctly identified the errors for that sample. Afterward the student inserts corrections for the circled words and keeps a record

Figure 4.1
Sample Error Reduction Chart—Spelling

Student's Name _____

Mark the number of errors found in a 300-word sample under the appropriate column.

				ERRORS			
DATE	2	4	6	8	10	12	14
9–1							
9–7							
9–14							
9–21							
9–28							
10–5							
10–12							
10–19							
10–26							

on a chart of the number of words for that week. In succeeding weeks similar selections are chosen with the same procedure.

At the teacher's discretion, he or she may dictate a 300-word paragraph containing words of special educational value. Students proofread and record errors as described above. The same technique may be used while focusing on grammar, sentence improvement, and so on.

LEARNING FROM ERRORS.   The old practice of having students write a misspelled word ten or twenty times has not proved very satisfactory. Despite the repetitions, it did not seem to make much difference for correct spelling in future compositions. In order for a writer to correct a misspelling, he has to develop some personal ways of overcoming the particular difficulty of that word.

One technique that has worked for many students is to capitalize the hard part of the word in a respelling exercise. A student circles the word that he has misspelled and then above the word rewrites it, printing in capital letters the letter or letters that he found confusing.

As an adjunct to that activity, it helps him even more if he will keep a list of troublesome words in a notebook or on cards. Each word on the list could be written with the hard letter or letters capitalized. For example, if a person wrote "I saw a horse runing down the street" the word in the notebook would be respelled "ruNNing." Thus the particular hard part is analyzed, identified, and respelled all in the same effort.

Along with capitalizing the hard part of the word, the student should be encouraged to think of any kind of memory device that will help him remember the correct spelling in the future. Those devices may be related to sound-spelling patterns or a mnemonic device that will jog his memory when he spells it again.

Additional spelling activities can be found in chapter 10.

REFERENCE

Fries, C. *Linguistics and Reading.* New York: Holt, Rinehart and Winston, 1962.

SUGGESTED READINGS

Cotton, K. *Effective Practices for Spelling Instruction: Literature Synthesis.* St. Louis, Mo.: CEMREL, Inc., and Portland, Oreg.: Northwest Regional Educational Lab, 1982. (ERIC Document Reproduction Service No. ED 219 788)
McCabe, Don. *Word Families.* Birch Run, Mich.: AVKO Foundation Publishers, 1978.
Wood, Margo. "Invented Spelling." *Language Arts* (October 1982): 707–717.

Chapter 5

VOCABULARY INSTRUCTION

Vocabulary instruction has two basic purposes: first, to help students learn the words they need in school, those that are essential to current topics and units of study; second, to develop interest and competence in learning words independently. Since we know that students' active participation in vocabulary development is necessary for meaningful learning to take place, student interest and curiosity are prerequisites for vocabulary instruction.

CAPTURING INTEREST IN VOCABULARY LEARNING

It is comforting to realize that students engage in word play quite naturally. Their interest in words includes jokes that play on double meanings, rhymes, riddles, and even talking in pig latin. Perhaps an awareness of words as "objects of interest" can spring from this natural playfulness. For example, a word categorization game may be used to involve students and heighten their awareness of words that are related in meaning.

As a starter, give students a list of words that includes some words they know and some they are about to study. The list needs to contain words that can be arranged in several categories. The following word list could precede a geometry lesson on angles. The students should be instructed to arrange the words in groups and think of a name for each group or category.

angle	isosceles	rectangle	diameter
square	circle	right angle	circumference
oblique angle	radius	triangle	obtuse angle

Students may work in groups or alone developing categorizations for these topic-centered words. The list of geometric terms can be categorized into words that involve circles, angles, or rectangles; it also can be grouped by figures that are round or angular, or figures that are closed or open.

Since we know that learning involves connecting the new with the known, categorization exercises provide a sound introductory vocabulary activity. The very act of establishing categories and comparing categories between students helps them call to mind their existing knowledge (word knowledge) before studying a lesson.

Setting Criteria for Effective Vocabulary Instruction

Vocabulary instruction needs to present students with well-organized encounters with words. It is not enough to meet a word once or to use it once in a word game. Vocabulary study includes making the word familiar enough so that it may be used in speaking and writing and understood in reading and listening.

The following criteria are appropriate for planning effective vocabulary instruction:

1. Words must be presented in context.
2. A variety of experiences with the same words is needed.
3. Strategies for remembering new words are essential.

Each criterion will be discussed in detail in the following sections.

PRESENTING WORDS IN CONTEXT

The contexts contributing to word meaning can range in size from small units, such as the immediately surrounding words, to large ones—the whole paragraph or passage. Students can literally use what they intuitively know about language and the information from context to determine a word's meaning in a particular setting. The following instructional strategies are appropriate for developing awareness of word context.

▶ **suggested activities**

DEFINITION WITHIN A SENTENCE.   Teachers can help students see clues to a word's contextual meaning by pointing out particular surrounding words that are helpful. In the sentence, "The *ancestors* of dogs were wild animals that lived outside," the context defines the word that is unknown. It is helpful to present vocabulary words in phrases to help students recognize the context as informative. The following examples indicate how significant words can provide contextual clues to meaning:

schools	Fish "schools" are simply groups of fish that stay together.
spines	A shark's skin has "spines" that are as sharp as teeth.

CLUES IN A PARAGRAPH.   As students read, have them list words or phrases that help define new words. For example, the meaning of a central word in a paragraph can be defined by the phrases the students underline. The example that follows illustrates this process.

Directions: Underline at least four words or phrases that tell what an amphibian is. Then list them.

Amphibians are animals that live double lives. Most live in the water when they are young. After they have grown up they live on land, although they return to the water to mate and to lay eggs. Amphibians are born with gills for breathing in water, just like fish. Later, most of them develop lungs for breathing air. Like fish, amphibians are cold-blooded. Their bodies have the same temperature as the air or water around them.

Contextual Clues

live in the water	have gills, then lungs
later live on land	cold-blooded

Have students develop a definition based on the contextual information they have gathered. In the passage above, *amphibian* would be defined as a cold-blooded animal that lives in the water and has gills when it is young, but lives on land later, breathing with lungs.

CLOZE PRACTICE.   Cloze exercises can be used to foster contextual awareness. They consist of passages in which every fifth or seventh word has been deleted. Students use their knowledge of context to identify deleted words. Contextual information at both the sentence and passage level provides clues for guessing words that are missing. By deleting every fifth word, the teacher forces the students to pay attention to language as well as patterns of thought.

As students work with cloze passages constructed from their science or social studies textbooks, their understanding of essential words defined contextually may increase; certainly they will become aware that they are using context to predict appropriate words and understand the passage as well. Lessons of this sort are more effective when selections of two or three hundred words are provided so that enough contextual information is available. Students get meaning from the passage as a whole as well as from immediate sentences.

SUBSTITUTION FOR WEAK WORDS.   Contextual knowledge is useful in improving student awareness of word choice in writing. By considering sentence and passage context, students can begin to identify words that are poor choices. Ask students to underline these "weak words," then study the context in order to find more meaningful substitutes.

Instruction can begin by having students work with a partner to consider underlined weak words from their compositions. The pair of students can look at the context to find the semantic features of the word that they need and then think of a new word to express those features. For example, in a passage describing a boy who *climbed* over a fence to get away from a vicious dog, the students might substitute the word *scrambled* for *climbed* in order to convey speed and the frantic quality of the moment. The students' notes might look like this:

> The boy climbed over the fence to escape the teeth of the vicious dog.
>
> Semantic features: hurry, speed, danger
> Revision: scrambled
>
> The boy scrambled over the fence to escape the teeth of the vicious dog.

PROVIDING A VARIETY OF EXPERIENCES

New words need to be repeated often before they become part of a student's vocabulary. Instructionally, several things can be done to help students understand and use specific words in listening, speaking, reading, and writing.

Before presenting a new vocabulary word in a reading selection, introduce that word in sample sentences that provide contextual clues to its meaning in the selection. Context is used as students discuss and predict word meanings. While reading the selection, students should be asked to identify the word's context. They can be instructed to write in a notebook a probable meaning for each new word encountered as they read, noting information about its meaning from the sense of the passage. The word and its associated meaning can then be discussed after reading and used in follow-up writing exercises.

Learning centers can be used to provide additional experiences with new vocabulary words. The following centers incorporate both reading and writing experiences.

Learning Centers

WRITING STORY REACTIONS.   Select a particularly interesting story (perhaps one from a supplementary reader) and place it in a learning center along with a posted list of vocabulary words that are important to it. Include a display area where students can post their written reactions to the story. These may include emotional reactions, simple opinions, or the sharing of a similar experience. Encourage students to use the new vocabulary words in the context of writing their reactions.

WRITING RIDDLES AND JOKES.   Establish two learning centers for new words, locating each on a particular side of the classroom. Post a list of the words at each learning center. One half the class uses one center, developing riddles to stump the other half of the class. Meanwhile the other half uses its center to develop riddles for the first group. Sample riddles should also be posted at each learning center. When each side is ready, the riddles from each group are posted in the opposite group's center. The centers themselves need to contain a posted list of current vocabulary words and a place to post riddles from the other group. The riddles and jokes might look like this:

What twinkles in the sunlight but hides in the dark?   (geode)

Knock, knock.   Who's there?   Arthur.   Arthur who?   (arthropod)

MAKING WORDS EASY TO REMEMBER

A number of strategies help students remember the words they learn. *Visual images* are useful for prompting memory. Simple sketches, no matter how crude, help children associate a word with its meaning. Students may keep individual illustrated word books to record important words and their definitions. Word books may be organized like a dictionary with each entry including the word, a statement of its meaning in the student's words, and perhaps a sketch and even a sentence or example of the word in use. For example, the word *diminutive* could have an entry including the following.

Diminutive

Means: very tiny
Opposite: very large
Example: a grain of sand
Use: The kitten looked diminutive next to the large cat.

Students may use their word books to review words previously studied (another way to increase memorability) and to spark their interest when they are thinking of topics and words for independent writing assignments. The word book, in essence, becomes a record of the student's deliberate effort to learn new words and use them in speaking and writing.

Relevance serves as an aid to memory. Making a word relevant to the students' world increases the likelihood that the word will be used. Students can discuss how a word relates to their recent experiences, tell what it means to them, and cite specific examples that connect the word to their world. Discussions of shared experiences can serve as material for students needing information before writing their own definition.

Word associations serve as yet another prompt to memory. If students pair one word with another (choosing perhaps a more familiar synonym) or associate it with a particular experience, the word may be more memorable. For example, if a student were trying to find an association for the word *pedestrian*, he might consider associations and experiences that develop a pairing. The thought process might proceed like this:

Target word:	*pedestrian*
Associations:	walk, sidewalk, crossing the street, "pedestrians cross here"
Experiences:	Cars have to stop so the pedestrians can cross the street.
Pairing:	pedestrian/walking

Mnemonic clues can help students remember words. Mnemonics are prompts to the memory, vivid cues that stick in the learner's memory and help in recalling a desired word. One kind of mnemonic clue is a word cue that plays on a particular aspect of a word in order to generate a visual image. For instance, the word *persuade* is remembered by associating it with the key word *purse*. Imagine, for example, two ladies shopping for purses and one saying, "I think you could *persuade* me to buy it" (Levin et al., 1982).

One way to construct a mnemonic clue is to find key words that not only sound like the word but also make the learner picture a funny visual image. Word pairs like *squall/squalus* (a genus of shark) are used to suggest funny pictures. The picture of a crying shark (a squalling squalus) is a visual image unusual enough to serve as an effective mnemonic clue.

Another (and perhaps simpler) kind of mnemonic is the paired visual image. Words are paired with pictures that depict memorable associations. For example, to remember the word *deport,* the learner might conjure up a picture of a ship leaving the harbor (port) with a person being *deported* aboard. The mental picture suggests the word's meaning.

Reviewing words seems to enhance their memorability. We know that spaced practice is an important aspect in helping students remember words. Certainly the additional information that is included in discussing review words increases memorability. Reviewing involves looking at previous information about the vocabulary word—its meaning, examples, sentences written using the word—and adding new examples. The review process may include reading the word, saying it, and writing sentences that use it in context.

Students with word books or systematic lists of vocabulary words studied previously can use the following routine for reviewing words independently.

Review Process

1. Say the word and think of its meaning.
2. Read sentences using the new word.
3. Write a sentence or example that includes the new word.

▶ **suggested activity**

C-S-S-D.   One mnemonic routine for figuring out new words is C-S-S-D. This strategy suggests the order in which specific approaches are used. The routine is as follows:

Context	Look at the *context* of the word and guess its meaning.
Structure	Study the *structure* of the word. Does its prefix, root, or suffix give clues to meaning?
Sound	*Sound* it out to see if you recognize the word from your speaking vocabulary. If the word is

a long one, try to sound it out in small parts, e.g., un-du-late.

Dictionary   Use the *dictionary* to determine the meaning. Match the context in which the word was found with the appropriate meaning.

Students only need to follow this routine until they figure out the unknown word. Perhaps context alone will provide enough information and other approaches will not be needed.

INCREASING VOCABULARY INDEPENDENTLY

Students must be able to learn words on their own, acquiring new vocabulary as they read and consciously trying to increase their vocabularies as they study. Instruction fostering independent word study, we think, needs to operate within the following framework:

1. *A variety of vocabulary strategies for independent learning must be presented.* Since students vary in their way of learning and remembering new words, exposure to a variety of strategies is appropriate.
2. *Deliberate effort on the student's part is essential for vocabulary growth.* Vocabulary growth can be accelerated by a conscious effort to remember particular vocabulary words and use them as often as possible.

▶ **ideas for student discussion and interaction**

As children read, encourage them to notice words that carry the main concepts. It also helps to have them write a central concept word on their notepaper as they read. That practice increases concentration and increases the likelihood that they will remember the words and concepts. After reading, students should consider what they have read and perhaps write a statement about each word, trying to catch its meaning. They can try to capture the main points of a selection by listing words that carry those ideas. The vocabulary of the selection, therefore, becomes an integral part of the learning that takes place. A conscious effort both to remember and to use the new words is required.

Figure 5.1
Sample Word Cluster

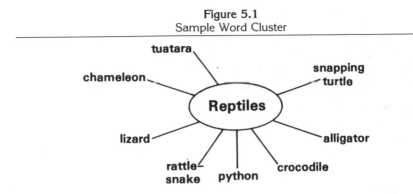

▶ **suggested activity**

WORD CLUSTERS.   Teach children to categorize words and expand meaning by clustering. Word clusters are developed by placing the main or central concept in the center of an imaginary circle. Branching from that central word are all the related words· that an individual or a group can generate. These clusters can be displayed on the chalkboard and later copied into student notebooks. As students build their own topical word clusters, they can use them to review concepts and to relate new words to familiar ones. Figure 5.1 shows a word cluster developed around the word *reptiles*.

Understanding New Words Independently

As students encounter new words independently, it is important that they develop a strategy for understanding them. The goal is to prevent unknown words from unduly slowing the flow of reading. Somehow the student needs to find a way to get meaning from the sentence or phrase in which the unknown word appears and also continue reading so that the meaning of the passage as a whole is not disrupted—when that is possible. Since students have a variety of approaches to accomplishing that end, ask them to share their techniques with each other. Questions like the following may be helpful:

- What do you do when you find a new word while reading?
- How do you determine the meaning of a new word without disrupting your reading?

- How do you know if the meaning you decided upon was actually appropriate?

Once the students have decided what they do when encountering new words in reading, give them a passage and have them observe whether their particular strategy actually works. Then have them describe again what they did when they came to the new word, what they thought about, and how successful their strategy actually was. Encourage students to revise their strategies to improve understanding while they are reading and after they have finished reading.

Students should understand that certain techniques can be applied during and after reading to help them determine the meaning of an unknown word. During the reading process, they can take a guess at the meaning. By looking at the words before and after the unknown word, they may be able to get a good sense from the sentence context of what the word means. After reading, they can look up the word in the dictionary. Again they must consider the context of the sentence when using dictionary definitions, as many words have multiple meanings. They must be sure the meaning they choose fits the use in the sentence.

Multimeaning Words

Students often experience difficulty studying words independently because they are unclear about words with multiple meanings. Words like *force* and *base* have a variety of meanings that are dependent on context. Students can "collect" these words and use them to reinforce their strategy of using word context to determine meanings. The collection of multimeaning words gathered by students might make an appropriate addition to the student's word notebook, particularly if each word meaning is illustrated. Lists like the following could be generated and used for study and review.

Love

Sometimes people fall in *love*.   (romance)
The score was *love*, fifteen.   (tennis score for zero)

Current

After the rainstorm, the *current* in the river was
   high.   (water flow)
The *current* time is 12:15.   (present)

USING PREFIXES, SUFFIXES, AND ROOT WORDS IN VOCABULARY BUILDING

When students study word structure, they learn to build new words using root words and affixes. This area of word study provides students with a sense of the relatedness of words, as one word becomes the key to understanding several others. Instruction in this area must focus on word meaning and be applied to reading and writing expriences where words with affixes are used in connected discourse. With these guidelines in mind, the following types of instruction are recommended:

1. Construct word families that relate various affixed forms of a word to its root word. For example, read: reading, readable, reread, misread, misreading.
2. Recognize words with affixes in reading and writing experiences.

Constructing Word Families

Word families help students relate words by structure and meaning. The word *joy* leads to *enjoy, enjoying, enjoyable, joyous, joyously,* and *joyless.* As students develop their own initial word families, they should confine their "family groupings" to actually existing words by using those that are found in reading or by using the dictionary to verify words they construct. Instruction can begin by selecting a word that appears with affixes in students' current assigned reading. Help students build a family of words related to the root word by using the following steps:

1. Write the root word.
2. Think about prefixes that can be added to the root word to build a new word. Write them in front of the root and underline the prefix.

3. Think about suffixes that can be added, write them after the root word, and underline the suffix.
4. Add additional related words as they occur in reading experiences.

A word family for the word *national* might include the following words:

*inter*national   national*ize*
*trans*national   national*ism*
*multi*national   national*ist*

Using this strategy, a student can build word families that contain words that occur later in reading and writing experiences.

·Simple lists of common prefixes and suffixes can be provided for students engaging in this activity. The following affixes have fairly consistent meanings and are appropriate for this activity:

Prefixes			*Suffixes*		
circum-	intro-	mal-	-able	-like	-ing
multi-	super-	sub-	-less	-ous	-ize
non-	extra-	mis-	-most	-ible	-acious

Words such as *function, read, ordinary, manage,* and *glamor* can be used to form some possible combinations. Of course, there are two dangers in this kind of lesson; first, that students will produce a wealth of nonwords, such as *disjoy* or *malcourage*; second, that they will focus entirely on words out of context. After a word-building lesson, present words with affixes in sentences and discuss the contextual meaning of affixed words. Sentences like the following would be appropriate:

The expert began to *deactivate* the bomb.
By *prearrangement*, the press arrived just as the celebrity got off the plane.

Recognizing Affixed Words in Reading

The transition from word building in practice exercises to word recognition in reading experiences is essential. Students can work out the meaning of affixed words found in their textbooks or in independent reading by using the following procedure:

1. Find the root of the word by removing its affixes. Think about the meaning of the root. The word *discontentment*, for example, can be handled by thinking:

   discontentment   dis-content-ment
   root: content   root meaning: happy

2. Add affixes to the root one by one, in effect reassembling the word and informally stating the new meaning with each addition.

   content = happy
   contentment = being happy
   discontentment = not being happy

3. Put the word back into its context to see if the tentative word meaning makes sense in the original sentence: "His sad face was a picture of discontentment." The phrase *sad face* fits with the word meaning developed for *discontentment*.

▶ **ideas for student discussion and interaction**

Show students a text passage like the following and discuss the meaning of the words with affixes that are included.

> After they moved to Chicago, each member of the Davis family went through a period of readjustment. John, who missed his old friends, was filled with discontentment. Ann learned to make new friends while renewing old friendships by writing letters.

Ask students:
- Are there any words with affixes in this passage?
- When you take the word apart by removing its affixes, what is the root word?
- What does the root word mean?
- When you add the suffix to it, how does the meaning change?
- When you add the prefix to it, what does the word mean?
- Does the word meaning developed in this way fit with the context of the sentence?

Encourage students to share their reactions to this strategy and have them suggest ways to apply it during reading.

▶ suggested activities

WORD DIAGRAMS.   To make word families more memorable (and perhaps more fun to study) introduce the idea of writing them on pictures. Show how the main word, written on one part of the picture, and the members of the word family, written on other less important parts of the diagram, fit together and are related in meaning and structure. Simple diagrams of objects such as a wheel, tree, octopus, or satellite, lend themselves to this kind of word diagram. A display of these diagrams may help make the word families more memorable.

THE LONGEST WORD.   Students who enjoy noticing long words in their textbooks may enjoy keeping track of who can find the longest word. To qualify, the word must be in one of the student's regular textbooks, included in a sentence, and not a proper noun. In order to score points (one for each letter in the word), students must write on a slip of paper the sentence in which the word appears and correctly write what the long word means in that context. A display area, perhaps a bulletin board, can be kept of all the players' names and their running totals. The long words can be listed after each student's name.

REFERENCE

Levin, Joel R., et al. "Mnemonic Versus Nonmnemonic Vocabulary: Learning Strategies for Children." *American Educational Research Journal* 19, no. 1 (Spring 1982): 124.

SUGGESTED READINGS

Beck, Isabel and Margaret McKeown. "Learning Words Well—A Program to Enhance Vocabulary Comprehension." *The Reading Teacher* 36, no. 7 (March 1983): 622–25.
Hafner, Lawrence E. and Hayden B. Holly. *Teaching Reading to Children.* 2nd Ed. New York: Macmillan, 1982, ch. 5, pp. 139–74.
Johnson, Dale D. and P. David Pearson. *Teaching Reading Vocabulary.* New York: Holt, Rinehart and Winston, 1978.

Chapter 6

BASIC COMPREHENSION

TEACHING READING COMPREHENSION

Traditionally, teachers have taught comprehension by asking questions after students have read silently. The assumption has been that such questions help students learn to gather information and grasp essential ideas. In fact, we know that when teachers ask a range of questions, such as recall, analysis, and judgment questions, students gain an awareness of the variety of information that can be gathered from a selection. The daily experience of being asked various questions and the observation that other students are able to answer them often stimulate students to read more intensely.

For some students, however, responding to questions is not enough. They need an explanation of exactly how to extract information from a passage. Teachers need to describe the thinking operations that are involved. These explanations can address the fundamental comprehension processes of recalling, analyzing, judging, and applying what is read. Teachers can develop step-by-step outlines that define and explain each process, conduct discussions where students talk through their own procedures, and use concrete demonstrations to help students understand each thinking operation. Demonstrations showing how judgments are made are particularly effective in providing a procedure for students to use in understanding how to think as they read.

In addition to focusing on thinking processes, comprehension instruction may center on strengthening specific components of comprehension. For instance, by increasing understanding of the vocabulary in a passage, comprehension can be improved. Teachers can show students how to understand vocabulary in the context of a story, apply techniques for remembering new words, and use new vocabulary in connection with concept development.

Comprehension is also improved by teaching students to look for connections between their existing knowledge and the new information encountered during reading. This can be achieved by discussing background concepts, as well as by skimming and predicting activities before reading.

▶ ideas for student discussion and interaction

Group discussions after silent reading provide an opportunity to help students develop comprehension strategies and learn from each other. For example, when the goal is to increase student awareness of the variety of information in a passage, recall, analysis, and judgment questions can be used. The discussion should begin with a rapid pooling of story information. Everyone contributes a bit of data or story detail. The next step is to ask a story analysis question. The teacher might ask how one event compares with another or what similarities there are between two characters. The teacher can ask students how they figured out their answers or where they found the information. Next, a question can be asked that requires students to make a judgment. It could ask which of the characters they would like to be or which event they would like to change. The point of the entire discussion can focus on the fact that different types of questions require distinct kinds of thinking and that a wide range of information comes out of reading a story when the reader is applying these various thinking processes.

▶ suggested activities

MAKING COMPARISONS.   In order to teach students to make comparisons as they read, a two-step lesson is needed.

1. Begin with a story that has two contrasting characters and a question that asks that they be compared. After students have read the story silently, discuss the question, stressing that comparison means bringing information together in order to see

likenesses and differences. Next, show students how to find the facts about each character and make actual lists for each one on the board or overhead. The two lists are compared by drawing lines to connect similar characteristics and students are asked to state the similarities and differences.

2. As a follow-through activity, ask students to write a comparison of two characters or events in another story.

SKIMMING AND PREDICTING BEFORE READING.   Connect students' existing fund of knowledge with the information contained in a new selection by teaching them to skim and predict.

Students can be presented with a factual article or a textbook passage and asked to skim it to gain a general impression of its subject matter. In addition to skimming the paragraphs, they may look at pictures, diagrams, subheadings, and the title.

Have students develop a two-column table with the headings, "My Predictions" and "What I Know." The first column entries predict what the selection is about and the second column entries relate what they already know about the subject. Students can be encouraged to record bits of prior knowledge and hunches about the subject as well as solid information.

Students may generate questions based on the information in the two columns and use them to direct their reading.

FINDING THE MAIN IDEA

Many students do not know what they are looking for when they attempt to identify main ideas. They lack a basic sense of what a main idea is and how it can be distinguished from other information. Instruction in this skill needs to provide concrete examples as a starting point. Simple demonstrations in which the teacher reads a passage and tells the main idea are useful. Students need to see main ideas underlined or written alongside a passage as a statement of the theme so they can gain an impression of what main ideas are. Diagrams may even be helpful for getting students to visualize the concept.

Once students have grasped the concept of main ideas, they need to understand the process of how to identify them. They need, in essence, to develop a personal strategy for approaching the thinking operations that are involved. It may help some students to see a step-by-step demonstration in which the teacher shows how to search for a sentence that states the main idea in a paragraph. Other students may learn best from their peers in discussions about how they determine the main ideas. The important point is that students need to understand that the task requires a particular kind of thinking.

▶ ideas for student discussion and interaction

An understanding of main ideas can be developed through discussions after silent reading. Plan a group of discussion questions that all lead to identification of the main idea. Relate each question to the central concept and help students gather information that points in that direction. The questions help students understand how to develop an appropriate line of reasoning in order to see the main concept.

In planning this kind of discussion activity, analyze the story and write a question for each major element that leads to the central concept. It may be helpful to see the questions as developing a line of reasoning, with each answer helping students deduce the main idea.

Another way to discuss main ideas is to have students share their strategies. The following five-step lesson can be used:

1. Students read the selection as a whole.
2. They skim it again and underline what they consider to be the most important information.
3. They look at their underlined information and decide what it tells about.
4. They write a main idea statement.
5. They discuss how they reached their decision.

The discussion has a "prove it" format in which the connection between the underlined information and the main idea statement must be shown. Ask students questions such as the following:

• How did you identify the main idea?
• What information supports your decision?

This discussion works particularly well when students are able to discuss why they underlined some information and did not select other information as being important.

A Sequence of Main Idea Lessons

A sequence of main idea lessons may be helpful for students who have little sense of how to proceed with a main idea question. The teacher should begin by reading a paragraph aloud and asking students to restate its message in their own words. The next step is to reduce the message to just one sentence, making sure the main idea is captured. This procedure can be repeated with several paragraphs.

Instruction can then move to tasks in which the student does the reading. As a first step, the teacher should show students how to select the sentence or phrase in a paragraph in which the author states his message. Students are required to choose among the sentences that are provided in order to show recognition of the main idea. The teacher needs to demonstrate how to make the choice by considering each sentence in reference to the paragraph as a whole.

Next, students may be shown how to read a paragraph and state the meaning in their own words, considering the total message first and trying to reduce the information to one central thought.

Further main idea lessons should help students work on inferring main ideas when they are not directly stated. The teacher can help students examine concrete information to make an inference, that is, to group related details in order to discover what they have in common.

By moving from simple to complex main idea lessons and showing students how to perform each task, a clearer understanding of main idea identification can be achieved.

▶ **suggested acitivities**

LISTENING TRAINING.   One of the ways to use listening training to teach main ideas is to have students listen to a short selection for the purpose of discussing the information they gather. The teacher can begin by reading a story orally. Students then

Table 6.1
Sample Groupings of Story Ideas

FACTS	MISSING ITEMS
Many items stolen	Money
House tightly locked	Expensive jewelry
Windows unlock from outside	Papers

PEOPLE WHO HAD KEY	APPEARANCE OF LIBRARY
Mr. and Mrs. Taylor	Furniture overturned
Cook	Papers on floor
Aunt	Male footprints outside open window

SUSPECTS AND MOTIVES

Mr. Taylor needed money.
The cook was a long-time
    friend.
The aunt was an invalid.

MAIN IDEA

The burglary was set up to look like an outsider did it, but actually no one outside the family could have gotten in.

retell the facts from their listening while the teacher writes them on the chalkboard or an overhead. After the main items have been written, students discuss which facts are similar. Information is then grouped by categories and a label decided upon for each group. The last part of the discussion should be to develop an overall main idea statement that includes each category. The example shown in table 6.1 might be produced during a discussion of a mystery story.

NEWSPAPER HEADLINES.   Newspaper headlines often give the main idea of the article and can be used to provide high-interest instruction. Select newspaper articles that appeal to students and have a clear central concept. Cover or remove the headlines and have the students read the article, think about its message, and write a headline of their own that states the main idea. Students having difficulty writing an appropriate headline can use the traditional journalistic questions *who, what, when, where, why,* and *how* to direct their thinking. The student-generated headlines can be compared to the original ones and any differences discussed.

WRITING MAIN IDEAS.   Students can learn about main ideas by writing them. For this activity, students work in pairs, exchange papers, and see if the main ideas they have written can be identified by their partners. The activity begins with a simple, one-paragraph writing assignment. Students are asked to tell about their favorite television show or some other familiar topic. The paragraph must include a main idea statement. Students write their paragraphs and exchange papers. Each partner's task is to underline the main idea and tell his partner the reasons for choosing that particular sentence.

TEACHING RECALL OF DETAILS

Students often approach reading as if it were a task in total recall and they were charged with retaining every possible bit of information. They engage in a sort of indiscriminate trivia search as they read, ending up with a jumble of information and a confused sense of what the story or passage was about.

To change students' perspectives, teachers can focus on the purpose for recalling details more sharply, helping students recognize that details are primarily useful in clarifying and supporting central ideas or concepts. Details can be used meaningfully to retell or describe important events in a story, predict coming events, or anticipate actions of characters. They also form the basis for reactions to a story.

Instructional activities that serve these purposes help students select meaningful details. For example, after students read a story and identify its important events, have them tell important details about each event. Students can use details to describe a character as well. The teacher should ask what was unusual about a character or what detail provided crucial information. In this manner, students use descriptive details to gain essential information.

The teacher can also ask questions that require students to make predictions based on specific data. Such questions might ask students to tell what they think will happen next in a story and give reasons for their answers. Furthermore, questions might ask which details help them predict what each character will do next or which details help them know how the story will end.

Students should be encouraged to use details to support their opinions about the stories or selections they read. They can be asked which character was the most interesting or which event was the high point of the story. They also can use details in making a critical evaluation of the story, telling what they did or did not like about it or why they felt it was effective or interesting. As students write or tell reactions, they can support them with important details so that recalling details becomes an integral part of the process of getting information from print.

▶ **ideas for student discussion and interaction**

In order to help students see the importance of details, a teacher should select a story that has a number of illustrations and conduct a discussion in which students focus on the details of the pictures and of the story itself. Before reading, have the students look at the first picture and describe what they see. Ask them to comment on the characters and predict what they will do. Next, the students should read the story and compare their predictions to the actual events. Ask them to discuss how the details and mental pictures they formed aided their answers.

▶ **suggested activities**

RIDDLES.   Students can make up riddles to describe central characters in the stories they have read. The riddles can ask, "Who am I?" and provide enough crucial details to give clues for the students who are guessing. These riddles can be used in a unit review or situation where a number of possible characters can be identified.

SUPPORTING AN ARGUMENT.   After students have read a story, they can write a paragraph that agrees or disagrees with a position statement offered by the teacher and written on the board. The statement should be one that would provoke disagreement. The point of the lesson is to help students see that details are useful in supporting an argument. The written arguments can also be used in a discussion of the story.

INTRODUCING . . . .   At the beginning of the year, the teacher and students can learn more about one another by writing a class book of introductions. The teacher and students each write a self-description containing important details about themselves, such as likes and dislikes, hobbies, best school subject, and so on. A photograph can be used to accompany the final composition. These pictures and writings are placed in a notebook and displayed in the classroom. The book provides visitors as well as students an opportunity to learn more about the teacher and pupils in the class. You can play a game of recall after the pupils have had a chance to read each other's self-descriptions. One student can announce, for example, "I know someone who likes baseball, is good in math, and has a brown dog." The person who is first to guess the correct person gets the chance to describe someone else.

SWAPPER'S FAIR.   This activity accompanies a newspaper unit since it involves students reading want ads. After reading and discussing ads from the paper, students write their own ads using specific details to describe items they want or items they have to trade. The finished ads are placed in a school newspaper or posted on a "Swapper's Board."

Combining Reading and Writing Activities to Enhance Recall

One new way to teach recall of details is to involve students in activities using both reading and writing. For example, as students read to recall details about a given character in a story, they can also note how details are used for descriptions. The descriptive paragraphs about characters can serve as examples that students refer to as they write character descriptions of themselves or of persons in their own stories. By looking at details from the perspective of a reader and a writer, students gain a richer awareness of how details are used to make descriptions more interesting.

The same approach can be applied to understanding the details that make an event exciting or a setting unusual. For example, students can read a story and answer questions that draw attention to the story's important details. They can apply the use of important details to their own writing as they create an original ending to a story they have read. The details in a story help suggest possible endings. Students should be encouraged to look at details to see what the setting was like, how the characters behaved, and what the author did to set up the final event. Following this sequence, teachers can help students learn to see and use the connection between reading and writing.

▶ ideas for student discussion and interaction

As students approach the task of writing an ending to a story, a preliminary discussion can be used to give them suggestions for getting started. First, they can trace the course of the events in the story and discuss possibilities for the outcome. The details of the story can be viewed as clues or hints pointing toward a probable ending. Second, students should be directed to look for information about the characters that are involved. The teacher can ask students to look at each character's actions in the past in order to predict his role in the final event. Details about character feelings and attitudes may provide useful information for students. Finally, the tone or mood of the story may be discussed. Teachers can ask what words the author used to convey the mood and what effect they had on the student's prospective ending. By the end of the discussion, each student will have gathered enough information to write an ending based on details found in various aspects of the story.

▶ suggested activities

READING TO OBSERVE A CHARACTER.   Instructional experiences that help students observe how characters are described can be useful in both reading and writing activies. Students may read a selection and pick one particular character to observe. The details that describe appearance, actions, moods, attitudes, and motives should be noticed. The teacher can help students see these details by framing questions about each and by having them list observations. Have students make four columns on a paper. The column headings should read: Appearance, Actions, Moods and Attitudes, and Motives. Under each column they list appropriate details. A character description of Rumpelstiltskin, for example, might look like this:

Appearance	Actions	Moods and Attitudes	Motives
long beard ragged clothes	makes people guess his name	angry when his name is guessed	wants to get a child of his own

After students have gathered data about their character, they should write a complete description. The descriptive paragraph serves as a word picture of their character and includes as many details as possible.

BASAL BRAINSTORMING.   Pick a story from the basal reader that contains several elements for students to relate personal experiences to or just to use their imaginations. Read the story with the class and then discuss it with them. Stimulate the students' ideas and thoughts by focusing on those offered or implied in the story. After students have gotten involved, have them write their own stories implementing one of the ideas mentioned during the discussion. Be prepared to offer suggestions for students having trouble thinking of an idea or having trouble getting started. The students should be encouraged to share their finished stories with their classmates. In this way, they are able to see how one passage (in this case a story) can provide different people with new and varied thoughts. This will help them to expand their personal expectations.

WRITING TO CONVEY A MOOD.   As students gain awareness of how details are used, their experiences can include lessons showing how mood is conveyed in stories. A good scary story can make this point vividly for students.

Begin by asking students to suggest words that are associated with a scary mood. These may be listed on the board or overhead for later reference. Next, read a frightening story aloud, having students listen for details that contribute to the mood. After the story, additional words that carry a mysterious mood can be listed along with the original ones.

HELPING FLUENT READERS RETAIN INFORMATION

Some readers approach reading assignments as if they were speed contests and prizes were being given for finishing quickly. These students seem to function without the expectation of retaining information. They simply race along, not really thinking about the text in front of them, only remembering certain highlighted details.

Instructionally, such students can profit from a number of approaches. The teacher can begin by providing specific purpose-setting questions before reading begins. The customary follow-up questions for reading lessons can be used in this manner and will help direct student reading. Preliminary discussions that develop necessary background concepts may be helpful as well, since the student who reads without retaining information may be one who lacks background to understand the passage. Such discussions should explain a concept in terms the student understands. An example would be describing the location of a story by comparing it to the general location where the student lives. The pre-reading discussion also might ask students to frame their own questions before reading—questions related to the background information that was provided.

Students who have trouble retaining information may profit from strategies that require them to answer questions after reading part of the selection. Provide two or three questions for students to answer at the midpoint and ask them to make a prediction about what will happen next. Another method is to have the reader retell the selection to a classmate; this may be helpful in focusing on retention and meaning. The teacher may also ask the student to read a page, close the book, and retell that portion of the text as a way of helping the student hold his attention for a short period.

Memory strategies can be used to help retention as well. By grouping details systematically, students may be able to remember important information. For example, have them list those details that tell the kind of person each character is. It may be useful for students to categorize information or develop simple associations that make information clusters easier to remember, as in events and people who appear in the opening scene. Visual associations that connect story information with an image or picture may be helpful, as students associate actions with a printed illustration. Whatever the combination of lessons, it is likely that a number of experiences will be needed to make a shift from fast, mindless reading to reading for meaning.

▶ **suggested activities**

READ AND REACT LESSONS.   A read and react exercise can be structured that will help the student read attentively. This procedure has the student read a short portion of a selection, usually two pages, then write a short reaction. The written comment may tell the student's opinion or thought about the story to that point, ask a question, or make a prediction. After the reader has recorded her reaction, she continues reading until reaching the next agreed upon stopping place. Again, the student records her reaction.

The class discussion of the selection as a whole occurs after all the students have completed their reading and have written their comments. In the discussion, students share their reactions for each stopping point, ask their questions, discuss answers, and state the predictions they made. By comparing the various reactions of students and discussing the story in terms of their opinions, students see the importance of thinking about the story as they read.

CONSTRUCTING VISUAL IMAGES.   Students who forget information rapidly often profit from strategies that help them picture a story. In order to carry out this strategy, the reader must first decide what he wishes to remember. It might be a sequence of key events or a single most important event in the story. Next, he thinks of a picture that captures the essence of the element he wishes to remember. Often visual images that are composites are constructed. Each part of the image represents an element of the story. If the visual image is an unusual one, an improbable picture, it will likely be memorable and will help the student recall the needed information.

TEACHING SEQUENCE OF EVENTS

Many students have trouble remembering the events in a story they have read. They recall the events at the end of the story and exclude what happened at the beginning. Sometimes they recall a jumble of happenings and neglect their order completely. By teaching students to recognize the sequence of events, a structure for ordering and recalling them is established.

Begin instruction in sequencing with listening training. Tell students to listen for the beginning, middle, and end of a very short story, then read the selection and have students tell what they remember. Write the remembered events on the board under the headings: Beginning, Middle, and End. Next, have students apply this sequencing framework on their own by reading a selection and identifying its parts. As students repeat this process on longer passages, they may realize that seeing the sequence or framework of a story helps them remember it.

Another way to help students recognize the sequence of events is to use story strips. Students read a story and write each event they remember on a story strip. The events can then be physically rearranged until they represent the order in the story itself. Students can thereby retell the story using the sequential story strips as a guide.

▶ **ideas for student discussion and interaction**

One way to discuss sequencing of events with students is to use cartoons. The teacher can pick simple cartoon strips with four or five pictures, cut them apart, scramble the order, and have students discuss how they can be arranged. Students need to see that the cartoon events follow one another in logical order. Ask students:

- Which event came first?
- Which is the last event? Why?
- What information is important for putting the pictures in order?

Further experience in sequencing can be provided by having students write a story to accompany a cartoon sequence. Students can write two or three sentences to tell the event in each picture. The total story they write must reflect the sequence suggested by the original cartoon.

▶ **suggested activities**

WRITING A SET OF INSTRUCTIONS.   When students write a set of instructions they often gain a sense of the importance of sequencing. They realize that the steps in their instructions cannot be followed in a random order, but must be followed in a specified sequence in order for the activity to be carried out properly.

To conduct this kind of writing lesson, have students think of a familiar activity that has several steps, such as playing hide-and-seek. Each student can write a list of the steps for completing his particular part of the game and write each step on a separate strip of paper. The write-up becomes a set of strips that students can exchange. Another student can read the strips, put them in order, and guess what the activity is. Possible subjects that lend themselves to this activity include how to make a peanut butter sandwich, carve a pumpkin, decorate a bicycle, or make a snowman.

ADVENTURE STORIES.   This activity begins with a reading experience. The students choose a partner and a book from the *Choose Your Adventure* series (1979–1982). This collection includes books by R. A. Montgomery, Edward Packard, and D. Terman, written for upper elementary grades. These books are written as if the reader were directly involved in and responsible for the adventure. The narrative is action-packed and presents a set of choices for the reader at the bottom of every page. The reader must choose the next course of action, thus determining the direction of the adventure. Each choice refers the reader to a corresponding page number. The reader turns to that page to continue the story. Here, once again, another choice must be made, and so it goes until the adventure comes to an end. The partners take turns reading and decide together the shape of their adventure.

After reading this type of book, the students work in groups to write a similar adventure story. The teacher divides the class into groups of eight. Each group decides on the characters, setting, and time for the story. The group then writes the beginning of the story making sure that the action leads to a choice (such as, should we go on, turn back, or wait for help). The group is then divided into two groups of four with each group taking one alternative and continuing the story. This write-and-divide process is repeated at various points as the stories progress, with the groups dividing to just two students, and then finally each student writes an ending to the adventure. Students experience writing in groups of eight, four, two, and finally alone. Support from the group experiences may make the individual writing easier. The final compiled writing may be bound and added to the library.

SUMMARIZING INFORMATION

In order to summarize a story, the reader must grasp the message, select its most vital elements, and restate it in his own words. The reader, in a sense, becomes a writer as he constructs his own shortened version of a story.

Students need to understand what a summary is and how it is different from simply retelling a story. Initially, students may regard a summary as a paragraph that explains the main ideas or events of a story and captures its central message.

Instruction may begin by having students read a story and divide it into three parts: the initial events, the middle (plot development), and the ending. Next, students should consider the main events in each section and write the most important ones in a few summarizing sentences. The story summary is then generated by combining the sentences from each section and comparing them with the story as a whole.

A simple underlining strategy may be useful for students having difficulty deciding what to include in a summary. Students should be directed to read a few paragraphs and underline the most important information. The summary can be written by including all the underlined items from the beginning, middle, and end of the story.

Other students may work best by outlining the story as a whole and then writing the summary. To assist students in developing their own outlines, a list of questions about the time and place of action, major characters, and basic plot could be used.

Whatever method students use to summarize information, they need to recognize that summarizing provides a way to organize information and remember key ideas.

▶ **ideas for student discussion and interaction**

Students often need to discuss first of all what a summary is—a boiled-down version of the original. The teacher can aid their understanding by having them discuss a story's summary and construct that summary in answer to a set of questions, such as:

- What is the point or the theme of this story?
- Who (which character) is involved in working out the main situation?
- Which event or events seem important to understanding the theme?
- How did it end?

Naturally, these questions need to be adjusted for the age and ability of the class, but such questions enable students to arrive at a summary by considering their answers.

▶ **suggested activities**

SUMMARIZING A STORY IN UNITS.   A story may be broken down into smaller units for students who find summarizing an entire story difficult. After each paragraph has been read, these students can write one sentence or a phrase that summarizes that particular paragraph or unit. When all of the paragraphs have been read, the list of sentences or phrases can be used to write a summary of the story as a whole.

ANOTHER VERSION.   For this activity the teacher needs to acquaint students with examples of books that have been shortened and adapted for younger children. The discussion in this lesson centers on ways authors adapt an original story in order to appeal to a younger audience. Students then choose a book to read and rewrite in a summary form. While reading the book, the students need to pay close attention to the characters, setting, and plot. In writing their shorter versions, the students must concentrate on preserving the meaning of the original book. The teacher can have conferences to check that each student comprehends the original storyline and to review the clarity and accuracy of the new version of the story. Once the teacher and student agree that the meaning of the original story has been re-created, revision for spelling and mechanics may be made. The final products can be bound and presented to a primary class for its classroom library or to the school library.

DEVELOPING BOOK JACKETS.   Students can write book summaries to interest classmates in a particular book they have read. These summaries can be made into illustrated book jackets for display in an interest center. Have students draw a picture for the book cover that represents a main event or idea in the story. The summaries themselves can be written on the inside flap of the cover. Of course, a display of book covers produced by students can be used to stimulate interest in reading.

NEWS SUMMARIES.   Students can prepare brief summaries of various news items to demonstrate that summaries are shortened versions of longer selections. To begin this activity, each student in a small group selects a news story from the front page of the newspaper. After reading the selection, the student writes a brief summary that includes the most important information in the article. After each member of the group has prepared his summary, the summaries themselves can be combined into a script and read in a manner similar to the nightly news on television.

REFERENCE

Choose Your Adventure series. Individual books by R. A. Montgomery, Edward Packard, and D. Terman. New York: Bantam, 1979–1982.

SUGGESTED READINGS

Cohen, Ruth. "Self-Generated Question as an Aid to Reading Comprehension." *The Reading Teacher* 36, no. 8 (April 1983): 770–75.
Eeds, Maryann. "What to Do When They Don't Understand What They Read— Research-Based Strategies for Teaching Reading Comprehension." *The Reading Teacher* 34, no. 5 (February 1981): 565–71.
Hennings, Dorothy Grant. "A Writing Approach to Reading Comprehension— Schema Theory in Action." *Language Arts* 59 (January 1982): 8–17.
Hodges, Richard E. and E. Hugh Rudorf (eds.). *Language and Learning to Read: What Teachers Should Know About Language.* Boston: Houghton, Mifflin, 1972.
Pearson, P. D. *Teaching Reading Comprehension.* New York: Holt, Rinehart and Winston, 1978.

Chapter 7

CRITICAL THINKING IN READING AND WRITING

FOSTERING CRITICAL THINKING

A number of activities in both reading and writing contribute to the growth of critical thinking among elementary students. When students form opinions about a story or evaluate information gained in reading, they are adopting a critical perspective.

Instruction in critical thinking is begun by simply having students read a story and state an opinion about it. Students can tell what they liked about the main character or what they thought of the story ending. They can tell what was surprising in the story or evaluate whether or not it was true to life. This kind of thinking is familiar to students and is as natural as talking about a movie or telling a friend about a television program.

The next step in instruction is to have students support their opinions with facts. Have them use information from their reading as evidence for opinions. Have them reread a selection and present data that prove their position. Ask them questions that require the use of their previous knowledge about a subject.

Questions such as the following will stimulate critical thinking:

- What are the facts in the story that support your opinion?
- How are the story characters similar to real people you know?

- What information in the story was new or surprising?

As students increase their ability to think critically, they can extend their skill by making evaluations. An easy way to begin this phase of instruction is to have students evaluate a story by comparing it to something familiar, such as other stories or experiences. Questions such as these may help students get started:

- What similarities are there between this story and others you have read?
- How are the events in the story like experiences you have had?

Comparisons can also involve fixed standards or agreed-upon criteria. For example, students could discuss criteria for evaluating story endings and agree that a good story ending brings the story action to a logical conclusion. (Some may be satisfied merely with "a happy ending".) Using that criterion, students could evaluate another story and discuss its ending. The criterion established in advance provides the basis for evaluation.

▶ **ideas for student discussion and interaction**

In a discussion, have students think about standards for evaluating a reading selection. If the selection is a news story, students can decide what kinds of information ought to be included. Begin the discussion by asking students to tell what they need to find out when they read a headline. Supply a specific example such as, Fire Destroys Shopping Center. Have students list the questions that are stimulated by the headline. After discussing the importance and effect of a headline, ask students to set a criterion for evaluating the news story. They need to decide what the function of a news story is and be specific about the standard for evaluating it. Their standard, for instance, might be that a news story must tell *who, what, when, where, why,* and *how.* Next, have students apply their evaluative standard to a news story of their choice and share their evaluation.

The point of the discussion is for students to read critically using a specific criterion for evaluation, and to realize that the reader needs to have something in mind in order to read critically.

► **suggested activities**

FINDING THE AUTHOR'S POINT OF VIEW.   Often students are unaware of the author's point of view as they read. To develop author awareness, choose a story or article that will produce a strong reaction in its readers and conduct the following four-step lesson.

1. Have students read the selection and tell what emotion it conveys.
2. Have them reread the story and underline words that express that particular emotion.
3. Ask them to imagine a contrasting emotion and substitute words in place of the underlined ones to carry that feeling.
4. Read the new passage aloud and discuss the change in mood.

As students see how words convey feelings, they can use that knowledge to recognize an author's purpose or point of view.

PERSONAL READING JOURNALS.   This activity provides students with an opportunity to write about stories from their basal readers. The teacher introduces the lesson by providing experiences to spur the students' interest and understanding; background knowledge and important vocabulary are discussed. Students then read the story silently. Immediately after reading, students write their reflections in their personal reading journals. This is a free writing experience without specific instructions, but students are generally encouraged to express their feelings and raise questions of personal interest. Students may also respond in other ways, such as writing another story with a similar plot or related characters, changing the ending, or writing what might happen next. Students may bring their journals to story discussion where they share their writings and raise questions for other students to answer.

WRITING STORY REVIEWS.   Students can exercise their critical perspective in a new way by writing story reviews. Rather than asking students to answer comprehension questions after reading a story, have them write a critical reaction to it. Show students what reviews are like by reading and discussing a review of a movie or television program. Mention that reviews often tell briefly about the story or program, state a reaction, and give examples to back up the specific reaction. Once the story reviews have been written, they can be displayed so that students can see how their reactions compared with those of their classmates.

EVALUATING WRITING.   (Students can apply critical thinking in evaluating their own writing.\ The writing lesson should be conducted as usual with attention paid to the prewriting, composing, and postwriting phases. After the composition is written, the students discuss procedures for evaluating their work. They can prepare a set of questions that will help them think critically about their writing, such as the following:

- Is the message clear?
- Does the composition stick to the subject?
- Are the sentences easy to understand?
- Is it interesting?

This list can then be used in self-evaluation and can serve as a guide in revision. Students can also exchange compositions and use the set of questions to critically read their neighbor's paper. This kind of activity serves double duty. Not only does it help students internalize what they need to consider when they write, but it helps students learn to think critically as well.

WRITTEN COMPARISONS.   Ask younger students to write as much as they can about a given topic (for example, science: the difference between plants and animals). Have them share their experiences and ideas with the rest of the class and add to their writings. After students have touched on everything they can think of, have them put these initial writings away until the end of the unit. Prepare reading and experience centers for students to use throughout the unit to test their hypotheses about their topic (for example, plant and animal characteristics). Discuss what they discover through reading and observing. After the topic has been thoroughly investigated, give students the same writing assignment that they began with. Have them compare their ideas before and after their unit of study and discuss the changes.

MEETING OF MINDS.   Patterned after the PBS program "Meeting of Minds," this activity helps older students recognize and think critically about differing viewpoints. Students begin by pairing up and choosing a pair of famous persons from the past or present to represent each side of an interesting and controversial issue. Students research their famous person's history and points of view, then write a hypothetical argument or discussion as if the character were speaking. Students may use a courtroom scene, debate, convention, or even a television interview as the setting for their discussion. For example, a debate in a state legislature could be the site of a discussion between Phylis Schlafly and Gloria Steinem on the rights of women. Such minidramas performed before the class will stimulate questions, discussion, and critical thinking.

TEACHING STUDENTS TO MAKE INFERENCES

Part of the relationship between reader and author involves making inferences. No author could possibly be explicit enough to provide everything his readers need. Instead, writers make assumptions and readers fill in the gaps, making inferences as they construct the message.

Making inferences in reading requires the reader to use his own information as well as the information on the page. A variety of situations in reading require inferences. For instance, they are needed to interpret titles, word meanings, event sequences, and tone in language. Figures of speech and rhetorical statements also need inferences for interpretation. When faced with missing information, whether a word or an event, a reader can often make inferences by building a "bridge" across the information that is available to arrive at a suitable solution.

Instruction in making inferences needs to provide two essential experiences. First, students and teachers need to discuss how inferences are made and see, for example, why one particular inference is more appropriate or logical than another. Second, students need to gather experience in making inferences themselves. They need to experiment with passages where inferences are needed.

Instruction in Making Inferences

Show students how to make inferences by conducting a demonstration with a specific story. Identify ahead of time some of the places where inferences are needed. Look, for example, for shifts in time and location. Begin by telling students that the point of the lesson is to learn how to fill in gaps during reading. That is, when they come to something that is not explained fully or is unclear, they will need to make an inference that fills in the needed information. Poetry, for example, is filled with inference opportunities. Carl Sandburg's line, "The fog comes on little cat feet," requires one kind of inference. Others are less complex: "The dog sniffed at the strange creature and backed away nervously."

Conduct the lesson as a listening activity by reading the story aloud in sections and have students listen for missing information. Read a section of the story and then ask students specific questions that require inferences. Questions such as these will be effective:

- Where is the action of the story taking place?
- What is the main character's reaction to the new event?
- Has the time of day changed in the story?

As the lesson proceeds, students will begin to see that their job as listener is to supply missing information. Emphasize that inferences are not wild guesses but logical answers based on the information at hand. Students then can think of their task as one of connecting ideas as they listen or read.

▶ **suggested activities**

INFERRING EMOTIONS. As students learn to make inferences in reading, their understanding of characters in the stories they read may be enriched. Students can think about the attitudes that favorite characters have, and can infer how changes in story circumstances affect the character.

Have students describe a particular character at the beginning of a story in terms of that individual's feelings, attitudes, and emotions. Then, have students tell the most important event in the story and infer the character's reaction to it. Students can describe the feelings, attitudes, and emotions that are present at the end of the story as well.

As students trace these changes, some of the information will be available in the story and some will be unstated. Help them to use their understanding of the character in order to make inferences.

INFERRING WORD MEANINGS.   Many of the words that seem to have definite meanings, in fact, require readers to make inferences. Words like *few, many, some,* and *near* gather their meaning from the context of the passage. Even some time-related words like *later* and *after a while* require the reader to infer specific meanings.

Have students reread a familiar passage and construct a list showing indefinite words and their meanings. Students can list an indefinite word in one column and write what they think it means in the other. A list like the following will be developed:

Indefinite Word	Inferred Meaning
few	less than five
later	in two or three hours

The essential element of this lesson is the insight that word meanings can be inferred and that information in the passage and in the reader's experience is important. Discuss with students how they decided on the inferred meanings.

TEACHING STUDENTS TO DRAW CONCLUSIONS

Activities that stimulate logical thinking serve as a good starting point for instruction in drawing conclusions. Students need experience in grouping related facts, seeing relationships, and comparing information. They also need to see the difference between logical and illogical thinking.

Listening activities are useful in getting students started. Have students listen while an exciting story is read. At various stopping points, ask students to predict what will happen next and encourage them to explain their answers. Provide examples of illogical conclusions so students can understand the kind of thinking that is involved and the kind to avoid.

In another type of exercise, present students with clusters of information and have them draw conclusions based on the data at hand. Data clusters could contain the facts from a news story, the details from a mystery, or even the description of a place. Each should end with a quesion requiring that a conclusion be drawn. Questions may be as simple as:

- How would you make the details fit together?
- What conclusions can be drawn?

The students' task is to see how the data are related and develop a logical answer that sums up the data in an appropriate conclusion.

It is also important that students gain experience in drawing conclusions from a story or article as a whole. Any newspaper article about a controversial issue of current interest provides the basis for useful discussions requiring logical conclusions. Mystery stories can also be used as materials for instruction. Whatever the materials, the important point is that students gain experience in the process of pulling information together and drawing their own conclusions.

▶ **ideas for student discussion and interaction**

By discussing current issues of interest, elementary students gain excellent opportunities to learn to draw logical conclusions. For older students, select a newspaper article that presents an issue with two sides. Ask students to listen for two purposes: first, to get the facts clearly in mind; second, to take a stand on the issue by drawing a conclusion. Read the article aloud and have students listen with care. Next, discuss the article and ask students specifically to tell the facts that support each possible position on the issue. List them on the board so that the data are available for all students. Urge students to look at the lists of information and take a position. By following this process, they learn to support their conclusions with reasons. Have students discuss their positions and try to persuade each other to see the worth of the opposing view.

For younger students, categorizing characters is useful. Have them sum up their sense of several characters and then explain why (based on actions or speeches) they drew those conclusions. A list on the board could clarify the discussion for primary-grade children.

Character	Label	Reasons
Isaac	fun-loving	played jokes on his friends
Karl	mean	chased the kids and said he would hit them
Nancy	silly	always giggled and didn't pay attention

▶ **suggested activities**

DRAWING CONCLUSIONS ABOUT CHARACTERS.   As a follow-up to a story read by the entire class, have students select their favorite characters. Put the names of these characters on the board and list everything about each character that they recall. After examining the list, have students draw a conclusion as to what kind of person each character was. Encourage them to go beyond the very general labels, such as "good," "nice," or "bad." Encourage them to be as specific as they can, indicating, for example, "She was helpful, but shy." Then, have each student write a description of one of the characters that expresses the conclusion he or she has drawn.

USING CONCLUSIONS TO SOLVE MYSTERIES.   Students can use their critical thinking skills to draw conclusions about the solutions to mystery stories. Select a mystery, such as an Encyclopedia Brown episode, and read the opening few paragraphs asking students to listen and predict what the episode is about. After predictions have been discussed (and perhaps listed on the board), read on until the central problem or mystery has been developed. Ask students to discuss the facts of the case. Have them first suggest solutions that are illogical and can be ruled out and then write a few logical solutions on the board. Finish reading the episode aloud, then compare the student solutions with the actual story solution.

RIDDLES ABOUT PLACES.   Have students write a description of a particular place, either real or imaginary, and include in the description enough details about what makes that unnamed place distinctive so that others can guess its identity. The location must be reasonably familiar to other students and special in some significant way.

The writer's task is to write in a few descriptive sentences enough information to make the place identifiable without making it too easy. Tell students that the reader of their description will have to draw a conclusion based on the information they give. They need to provide enough information so that the appropriate conclusion can be drawn.

TEACHING STUDENTS TO DISTINGUISH BETWEEN FACTS AND OPINIONS

Before students can distinguish between facts and opinions as kinds of information, they need to have the characteristics of each category solidly in mind. Facts are statements about what happened or what was done. They represent real events or verifiable information. On the other hand, opinions are beliefs or judgments that tell what a person thinks about the events that happened. They are based on a person's judgment or feelings.

These distinctions are useful to students learning to think critically. They are essential in evaluating any selection that attempts to persuade or make sense for a certain set of ideas. Students need to know how to sort facts from opinions before they can interpret information from their reading.

Begin instruction by having students read a common selection and find the facts it presents. These can be written in a column on the board. Next, have students state their feelings about the events in the story. They can react to the story, offer a judgment, or tell what they think about it. List these in another column using the following format:

Facts	Opinions
(what happened)	(what I think about it)

Discuss the differences among the items listed in the two columns and help students see the contrast between the two kinds of statements. It is important that the value of both categories is recognized since each represents a useful kind of information.

Older students can listen as a news story from a newspaper is read aloud and a related editorial on the same subject is read.

Ask students to tell what the purpose of each selection is and give examples of specific facts or opinions from each.

Younger students may proceed to articles where both facts and opinions are presented together. The *Mini Page* feature from the newspaper often represents that kind of writing. Persuasive articles usually provide such a mixture and are interesting to students. Have students read and discuss the facts and opinions the article presents using questions such as these:

- What was the author's purpose?
- How were the facts determined?
- What were the most persuasive opinions?
- What were the most important facts?
- What is your response to the article?
- Are you persuaded by the author?

The point of this instruction is for students to understand the differences between facts and opinions and to grasp how each is used to convince the reader.

The distinction between facts and opinions can be made more vivid through an activity involving drama. Choose two or three students to stage a brief drama, for example, a scene from a popular movie or a startling incident. While the drama is being planned, divide the rest of the class into two groups: reporters and feature writers. The groups will have different tasks. The reporters are to write the facts and the feature writers are to express opinions about the event. Next, stage the event and have each student write an account of it according to his or her role. After writing, allow students to exchange papers with a person from the other group. Students can observe the differences in what was written and judge whether the students from the other group fulfilled their assignment. Discuss these differences and have students notice how their observations and opinions vary.

▶ **suggested activities**

FACTS VERSUS OPINIONS.   Both reading and writing activities should be provided as students learn to make the distinction between facts and opinions. The following two-part lesson makes that connection.

1. Have students read an article and list two or three of the most important facts that it presents. Discuss with them the source of the information and try to determine whether the facts were gathered by observation or by some other means.

2. Have students write their own opinion of the article. Discuss the difference between facts and opinions in terms of their sources.

FINDING FACTS AND OPINIONS IN THE NEWSPAPER.   Have students look at the newspaper for articles that contain a mixture of fact and opinion. After each student has selected an article of particular interest, have him read it and underline statements that are opinions of the writer rather than statements of fact. Have students react to the article by answering these questions:

- What did you conclude from the article?
- Was your conclusion based on fact or opinion?

Students can use these two questions with news stories and feature articles from the newspaper or from children's magazines. They can decide which part of the newspaper is most concerned with fact and which with opinion.

FINDING FACTS AND OPINIONS IN ADVERTISEMENTS.   Since elementary students are exposed to a great deal of advertising as they watch television and look at magazines, the analysis of advertisements is appropriate as the focus of instruction. The language of commercials forms a significant part of the daily intake of information that many students receive. They need to realize that advertising has a purpose: to inform, persuade, and create need. Have students look critically at advertisements and ask:

- How much of the information in a commercial is true?
- Which part is trying to persuade me to use the product?
- Are opinions of famous people used in ads? Why?

Have students find an advertisement in a magazine that presents both facts and opinions. Students can underline the facts, circle the opinions, and tell what part each plays in the total message.

LETTERS TO THE EDITOR. Writing a letter to the editor in response to an article, editorial, or another letter is one way to involve students in both reading and writing. To understand the context in which such letters are published, have the class examine the editorial page of the newspaper. Then give students a copy of a current letter to the editor that discusses an issue relevant to their experience. Letters concerning the quality of education or the closing of schools can serve this function. After students have read the letter, discuss its ideas in terms of whether fact or opinion (or both) is presented. Have students break into small groups to write a letter in reply. Each group's rough draft is shared with the class as a whole so that all opinions are discussed. Finally, compose a class letter combining ideas in all the rough drafts. The completed letter may be sent to the newspaper for possible publication. (In the event that there are major differences of opinion, help the students to come to a consensus as they combine their letters; or if more than one view is valid, you could send more than one letter.)

FACT AND OPINION IN MAGAZINES. Many magazines and weekly tabloid newspapers, particularly the kind available at grocery store check-out counters, contain both fact and fiction so tightly interwoven that careful scrutiny is needed to identify the actual information. Choose an appropriate article from one of these publications and have students read it and discuss its content. Students should identify specific points in the article as examples of fact or opinion and support their claims with concrete information or with statements about needed information. Once most of the information in the article has been discussed, the class can consider how credible the article is and attempt to establish a standard of credibility based on the proportion of fact and opinion.

TEACHING STUDENTS TO COMPARE AND CONTRAST INFORMATION

One of the ways to critically evaluate information is to compare it to related information that is already familiar. Comparisons provide a yardstick or standard for judging a new story or piece of information. Students already know a great deal about this thinking skill, since they make comparisons every day. When they talk about television shows and note that the adventure programs on Thursday are better than those on Friday or that one subject in school is more interesting than another, they are using this skill. The instructional task, then, is to teach students to apply this technique to their reading and writing experiences. Students can make a relative statement about how exciting a story is by comparing it to a similar story that they liked. The comparison gives them a concrete way to make evaluative statements about stories and suggests a structure for the discussion.

Similarly, the act of contrasting information suggests that two related items are scrutinized in order to see their differences. For example, a student can explain an event by telling how it differed from a corresponding one.

Instruction in comparing and contrasting requires that students learn to bring together similar kinds of information and see relationships. Start instruction by having students compare one character in a story with another. Students can look at similarities and differences by discussing questions like the following:

- Do the two characters look alike?
- How are their interests similar?
- What problems do the two characters have that are the same?
- How are the feelings of the characters different?

Continue instruction by having students compare and contrast related stories. The structure of the story (that is, its beginning, middle, and final events) can be referred to in making the comparison. Questions such as these are appropriate:

- Were the locations of the stories alike?
- In what ways were the beginnings of the two stories different?
- Which events in the middle of the two stories were the most interesting?
- How were they similar?
- How were the story endings different?

Students may express personal evaluations as they draw comparisons and contrasts. Have students evaluate which character they liked best or least and compare that character with another. Have students tell which story event they thought was the most exciting and contrast it with another exciting event.

These activities lead students to another way of thinking critically. They suggest that information can be explained and sometimes evaluated effectively by comparing and contrasting it with similar kinds of information.

▶ **suggested activities**

SAME OR DIFFERENT?   Young students can sharpen their observational powers as well as their ability to quickly frame comparing and contrasting statements through the following game. Prepare two stacks of large, randomly arranged pictures. They may include pictures of people, places, animals, shapes, or anything interesting to children. Divide students into two teams and have each team in turn draw two pictures from the stacks, and state how they are the same and/or different. A team point is scored when an acceptable comparing or contrasting statement is made by any team member.

To extend the activity after the game, the participants choose any two pictures and write two or three sentences telling how they are the same or different. These sentences can then be tacked under the pictures on the bulletin board.

COMPARING DESCRIPTIONS.   Have each student make a list of four to five items that tell about himself, such as age, sports, hobbies, number of brothers and sisters, what he likes to do after school, and what books and television programs are his favorites. Next, he should make a parallel list telling the same categories of information about another person that he knows. The contrasting person could be a brother or sister, close friend, classmate, or even a character in a story. The students then may use the two lists of information to present orally or in writing a comparison telling the similarities and differences between the two descriptive lists. A sample list might look like the following:

About Me	*About My Sister*
5th grade	always talking to friends
like sports	plays on a basketball team
quiet and serious	7th grade
like books	reads a lot
play chess	noisy

Similarities: We both like sports and read.
Differences: I am serious and quiet but my sister makes a lot
  of noise.

UNDERSTANDING CAUSE-AND-EFFECT RELATIONSHIPS

An awareness of cause-and-effect relationships enables the reader
to see connections between events in a story. It allows him to
anticipate a coming event because he sees it as a logical result of
a previous one. It helps him think critically about the actions of
characters since he can link their actions to previous ones.

Instruction can begin with a warm-up listening activity. Tell
students to listen as a sentence is read and have them suggest an
outcome or possible result. Use sentences such as the following:

The tornado headed right for a neighborhood with tall trees.
We forgot that the cookies were baking in the oven.
The zookeeper forgot to lock the door to the monkey's cage.
The mouse spotted the cheese that was held in the trap.

In each of these statements, the situation is the cause, and the
predicted event is the effect. Show students how cause-and-effect
statements are linked. Complete a list like the following on the
chalk board, giving the students the cause and letting them give
the effect.

Cause	*Effect*
tornado hits	trees fall
forgot cookies	cookies burn
cage unlocked	monkey escapes
cheese in trap	mouse caught

Now see if students can find the cause if they are given the effect. Ask them to listen and guess the cause for each of the following:

We missed the bus.
Mud was tracked all over the room.
We couldn't unlock our own car.

Again, record the students' answers in a cause-and-effect table so that the linkage is clear. Write the effect first and have the students give the cause.

Cause	Effect
overslept	missed bus
muddy boots	mud tracked
keys locked in car	can't unlock car

Explain that events in a story are often linked together by cause-and-effect relationships. Have students read a story to find these relationships. Stress that the link between cause and effect can be tested by asking these two questions:

- What caused this event to happen?
- What happened as a result of this event?

Discuss the links that students have found and help them select events that fit the cause-and-effect pattern.

Next, show students that they can use their knowledge of cause-and-effect relationships to predict coming events in a story. In preparation for the lesson, analyze a story for its cause-and-effect relationships and establish fixed stopping points from which students can make effective predictions. Have students read to a designated point, describe the situation in the story, then predict a likely result. Discuss student predictions and have students continue reading to see what happens next. They may realize that story events are often the logical result of previous actions. This kind of critical thinking helps students understand why events happen and anticipate what will happen next.

The actions of story characters can also be studied by looking for cause-and-effect relationships. Students can think of a character's motive or main intention as a possible *cause* of his actions. The actual events or things the character does can then be thought of as outcomes of that intention. They are the result or *effect* of the original motive. By using this cause-and-effect relationship, students can think critically about the actions of story characters.

▶ **ideas for student discussion and interaction**

After students have listened to the first part of a story, have them decide what the main character thought was most important. Discuss the main character's motive, allowing students to tell their ideas. List the motive on the board. Next, ask students to listen to the rest of the story to see what happens as a result of the character's motive. Ask them to determine what effect the motive or intention had on the character's actions.

Allow students to share their ideas and list the actions that students suggest as evidence of the character carrying out his intention.

▶ **suggested activities**

FINDING CAUSE-AND-EFFECT RELATIONSHIPS IN READING SELECTIONS.   After participating in discussions and activities involving cause-and-effect relationships, have students read a story and analyze its main event in terms of cause-and-effect relationships. The following steps will be helpful:

1. Read a story silently and notice which event seemed to be the most important.
2. Think about a main event and decide what caused it to happen. Consider actions of characters as well as conditions in the story.
3. Think about the results of the main event. What effect did it have on the events that followed?

USING CAUSE-AND-EFFECT RELATIONSHIPS TO MAKE PREDICTIONS. Students can use cause-and-effect relationships to predict what will happen next in a story. Have them read to the point just after the first event in a story. Ask them to predict the next event by asking:

- What will happen next?
- What is its cause?

Have students continue reading and notice what actually did happen in the story. As students continue reading, have them find places where they can predict the next event by thinking about its cause and guessing what a reasonable result or effect would be. Have students write these causes and predicted effects in lists so they can share them in discussion.

SUGGESTED READINGS

Atwood, Beth S. "Critical Reading: A Social Experience." *Learning* 4 (1975): 34–37.

Hunkins, Francis P. *Questioning Strategies and Techniques.* Boston: Allyn and Bacon, 1972.

Lundsteen, Sara. "Levels of Meaning in Reading." *The Reading Teacher* 28 (1974): 268–72.

Newkirk, Thomas. "Young Writers as Critical Readers." *Language Arts* 59, no. 5 (May 1982): 451–57.

Chapter 8

STUDY STRATEGIES: HOW TO LEARN AND STUDY EFFECTIVELY

A number of study strategies are helpful for elementary students. Some involve learning how to learn: learning to follow directions, concentrate, and clarify information. Other strategies involve learning how to study: finding information in references, adjusting reading speed for various purposes, and reviewing to retain information.

LEARNING HOW TO LEARN

The process of learning how to "tune in" and concentrate is of special importance for elementary students. When this skill is applied to specific reading tasks or used while writing, it enables students to focus their attention.

A simple self-monitoring strategy can help students get started. Have students approach each lesson by asking themselves, *What is this lesson about?* They need to be able to identify the lesson's purpose and have a clear idea of what they are studying. Next, have them ask, *What am I supposed to do?* and clarify the directions so they are certain about how to proceed. Have students answer both questions in their own words before beginning a lesson. The two questions can be printed on bookmarks or reminder cards to help forgetful students.

Next, help students focus their attention while they are working. Students can become aware of "tuning in" to their task. They can monitor themselves by asking, *What am I thinking about?* and when they find they are thinking about something other than the lesson, they consciously "tune in" again. By refocusing in this manner, students get themselves back on task without further attention to distractions. Some people also find it helpful to read with a pencil in hand, making random notes as a way of keeping on target.

Learning to clarify information is another aspect of learning how to learn. Students need to distinguish between understanding a lesson and not really grasping it. In discussing this with students, specific techniques need to be mentioned for each of the following questions:

1. How do I know that I understand the lesson? What evidence is there?
2. What can I do if I do not understand?

Self-Checks: Gathering Evidence of Understanding

Students need specific strategies for testing understanding on their own. These could include:

1. Closing the book and telling the concept to oneself to see if it makes sense.
2. Trying to answer the questions at the end of the chapter.
3. Writing one or two sentences that tell the main point of the lesson.
4. Listing the main elements of the concept.
5. Drawing a simple diagram of the concept (see, for example, figure 8.1).

Once students have identified ways to test their understanding, they need to develop a set of strategies to use when they do not understand. This may include developing questions that help clarify confusing sections or rereading the unclear sections.

Generally, these strategies for learning how to learn and the more traditional strategies for learning how to study constitute an essential part of the elementary student's training. They are

Figure 8.1
Simple Diagram of a Concept

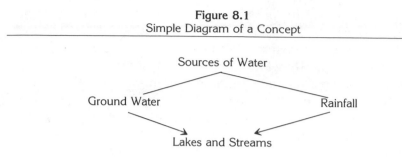

the study skills that help readers gain independence as learners and equip them for the task of reading to learn.

▶ ideas for student discussion and interaction

Demonstrate how to study a textbook passage with the following listening lesson and discussion. Ask students to listen to a selection and be ready to talk about it in their own words. Use a passage from a science or social studies text, selecting a somewhat unfamiliar topic for the lesson. After students have listened to the passage, conduct the following steps:

1. Have them retell the information from the article and suggest important items to be listed on the board under the heading, Summary of Information.
2. Discuss the article enough to help students identify areas where their understanding was inadequate. List these items (again suggested by the students themselves) on the board under the headings, Unclear Areas.
3. Ask students to think about each unclear area and develop a question to investigate it. List these questions under the heading, Related Questions.
4. Taking one question at a time, locate the portion of the text that discusses that issue. Reread the text and discuss its information, trying to answer the question that was posed.

The foregoing lesson can be applied as an independent learning strategy as well. When students are studying independently, have them read the assigned passage twice—first to gain a general sense of its information and then to go over the sections where information is unclear. Students can routinely use the three headings from the discussion to help them work independently. By learning to summarize information, identify unclear areas, and develop questions, they will internalize a method for clarifying concepts in their readings.

▶ **suggested activities**

READY, SET, GO.   One way to help younger students prepare for a lesson is to make them familiar with both its purpose and specific instructions. Have students listen as a lesson is introduced and instructions are given. Then, review the information by asking students to retell it silently to themselves using the following format:

Ready: Tell what the lesson is about.
Set: Tell the directions or instructions.
Go: Begin.

DESTROYING DISTRACTIONS.   Explain that distractions simply make it difficult to work and have each student consider what he can do to destroy the distractions that particularly bother him when he studies at home or in school. Students may suggest, for instance, ways to ignore the T.V. or cope with a pestering little brother. Students can also talk about ways to improve concentration. For instance, better concentration is produced when students work for a short time and then take a break or shift to another activity. Students need to recognize that everyone experiences times when his concentration is poor. Ask students to share suggestions for staying on task, even when it is difficult to concentrate.

After ideas have been exchanged in discussion, have each student write his plan for destroying distractions. The plan may take the format of the following list, with entries under Persistent Distractions being problems and entries under Destroyers being solutions.

Persistent Distractions	*Destroyers*
Too much noise in my room.	Make everyone leave.
Television is always on.	Find a room away from the T.V., or turn T.V. off.

FOLLOWING DIRECTIONS

Students often skip directions rather than reading them. Their strategy is to begin working on an assignment and figure out the directions as they go along—besides, the teacher will explain if asked. Of the students who do read directions, many have difficulty translating them into a course of action. They cannot decide what to do first or how to interpret directions as a step-by-step procedure.

Restating Directions

There are a number of approaches that help students improve in following directions. Students at every level can be taught to recheck directions before beginning a lesson. They may put directions into their own words orally or rewrite them as a series of steps. The restatement serves as a verifying procedure before beginning to work independently.

Verifying directions and restating them accurately can be considered part of each regular assignment. Begin by giving the directions for each lesson orally in the usual manner. Tell the students to write the directions in their own words at the top of their paper. Give two grades for the lesson: one for accuracy of directions and another for work on the lesson itself.

Listening to Directions

Listening exercises are also effective in training students to understand directions. Have students complete a small project by following step-by-step directions. For example, give students a set of geometric shapes: a circle, triangle, square, and rectangle. Have them arrange the shapes in a design by following oral directions. Accuracy in following directions can be checked by comparing the student's arrangement with the proper arrangement. The instructions can be as simple or as complex as appropriate. For example:

Simple Directions

1. Put the circle on top of the square.
2. Put the triangle on top of the rectangle.
3. Place the rectangle on the right side of the square.

Figure 8.2
Arrangement of Shapes According to Simple Directions

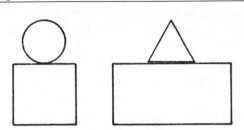

The proper arrangement would be as shown in figure 8.2.

Complex Directions

1. Arrange the figures in a line by putting the circle on the left and the triangle on the other end.
2. Put the square next to the circle.
3. Place the rectangle between the square and the triangle.

The proper arrangement would be as shown in figure 8.3.

Writing Directions

To augment the listening exercises, instruction in writing step-by-step directions can be included. Have students develop their own arrangement of shapes, then write a set of directions that will help a partner construct that arrangement. Students need to list all the steps and present them in a reasonable order. The adequacy of the directions will be shown by the design that is made.

Once students have learned to write a set of step-by-step directions, they can discuss how to understand written directions when they appear in paragraph form. Students often have difficulty with long written directions because they cannot translate them into substeps and are unable to find a starting point for the procedure.

Figure 8.3
Arrangement of Shapes According to Complex Directions

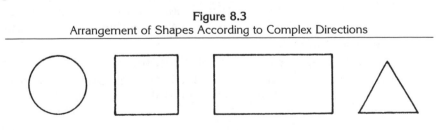

For instruction in this area, select a lengthy written direction from one of the texts the students ordinarily use. Help students simplify the directions by showing them how to list the separate steps that are included. The following directions are helpful to tell students:

1. Read the directions as a whole.
2. Reread them to find the separate activities and mark a slash between one activity and another.
3. Arrange the activities in list form.
4. Verify that the steps are in logical order.
5. Compare the original directions and your list of steps to see that the simplified directions are complete.

Implementing Directions

The process of understanding directions includes more than merely grasping their meaning, it requires that students translate them into an appropriate course of action. Teachers can help students implement directions successfully by having them use the following strategies:

1. Follow directions one step at a time, checking back with the directions after each step.
2. Refer to the directions whenever there is a question about what to do next.
3. Review finished work by referring first to the directions and then to the actual work that was completed.

▶ **suggested activities**

MYSTERY DIRECTIONS (FOR YOUNGER STUDENTS).　　Ask younger students to write a set of directions for drawing a familiar animal. They must consider what part should be drawn first and what other parts need to be mentioned, such as ears, tails, horns, stripes, and so on. They also need to tell what view (front, side) they are describing.

Have students write the set of directions in sequential order and give them to a partner. The partner must not know what animal he is trying to draw. He simply follows the directions and guesses what animal it is. Of course, the partner must not draw any part that is not included in the directions. The success of the directions will be revealed in the drawing that is made.

MYSTERY DIRECTIONS (FOR OLDER STUDENTS).   Ask older students to work alone constructing a specific object or figure out of modeling clay (for example, a snake-like object or one that looks like a snowman). Urge them to make the clay figure out of shapes they can talk about, such as cylinders, cubes, or spheres. Then have them write a step-by-step set of directions for constructing that arrangement. Students need to check their directions against the model, making sure they include every element needed.

When the directions are complete, the student covers his own clay figure, chooses a partner, and hands him a chunk of clay and the set of directions. The partner tries to make the figure using only the written directions. The author of the directions serves as observer (perhaps adding an instruction or two to the directions). At the end, the two students compare their clay models, seeing how similar they are and discussing the set of written directions.

WRITING SEQUENTIAL DIRECTIONS.   Have students select an activity that they know thoroughly, such as getting ready for school, making a special kind of sandwich, or playing a particular game. Ask them to think about it long enough to identify all the information that needs to be included in a set of directions for that activity. They can jot down words to suggest important information. Have them decide how to start the activity and write an instruction for the first step. Next, have them list the steps that are needed to carry out the rest of the activity. Check the sequential order to see if it is logical. Next, cut the sentences into separate strips, so their order can be mixed up.

The effectiveness of the directions can be checked by giving them to another student in scrambled order. Have the student unscramble the directions and identify the activity.

LEARNING HOW TO STUDY

As students begin the process of reading to learn, a new kind of reading material gains importance. Students need to use dictionaries, encyclopedias, and library reference works as sources of information. This expansion calls for instruction that keeps interest high and makes using new materials as comfortable as possible.

For example, making dictionary study comfortable for young children suggests that study be confined to two simple tasks: (1) locating important words and (2) determining their meaning. Other features of dictionaries, such as using pronunciation keys and recognizing elements of the dictionary entry, can be emphasized later.

To keep early experiences with encyclopedias comfortable, initial instruction can focus on helping students find information and use it appropriately. This introduction allows the teacher to focus on a problem that often arises as students begin using encyclopedias: students tend to copy the entries word for word. Of course, students need to put information into their own language to generate their own reports. They need, it seems, instruction in how to use encyclopedia information appropriately. Instruction can focus on two tasks: (1) locating information about a topic and (2) using information from encyclopedias in simple writing tasks.

Locating Information in Dictionaries and Encyclopedias

This initial phase of instruction has two important functions: (1) to help students find the information they are looking for and (2) to stimulate independent exploration. Our concern about guide words and indexes and how children can be taught to use them accurately must not interfere with the pleasures of simply exploring in dictionaries and encyclopedias and finding new information. Children's curiosity is a powerful motivator and ought to be captured in the kinds of instructional activities we plan. Children need time, for instance, to look at the sketch of the gorilla that appears on the same dictionary page as the definition of the word *gorge*.

Getting comfortable with dictionaries can begin very simply with a four-step lesson to locate a target word.

1. Find the *section* in the alphabet (beginning, middle, or end) of the first letter of the word. Turn to that same section in the dictionary.
2. Find the *pages* that begin with the first letter of the word.

Figure 8.4
Sample Guide Word "Gate"

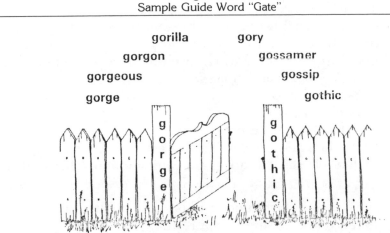

gorilla   gory

gorgon   gossamer

gorgeous   gossip

gorge   gothic

3. Find the *guide words* that include the target word.
4. Find the *word* by skimming the dictionary page.

Often students have trouble understanding how to use the
guide words. It may help to tell students to think of them as
"gates." Students can look for the right gate in order to find the
page that includes their word. Some students may even need to
picture this idea and practice choosing the right gate to grasp the
concept of guide words. Figure 8.4 depicts the gate that could be
imagined for the guide words *gorge* and *gothic*, which were encountered while searching for the word *gossamer*.

Students may also need help learning to skim down the page
to find their word. Tell them to watch as they move their finger
slowly down the page and look at the words by their finger. This
helps to eliminate the frantic searching that many students do
even after they have found the right page.

After students learn to find a word easily, they are ready to
use a dictionary entry to find an appropriate meaning. It is often
confusing to children to find two or three meanings in a dictionary
entry for a single word. Try this approach to help students:

1. Start with the target word presented in the context of a
   sentence. Example: The spider's *gossamer* web twinkled
   with dew.

2. Ask students to think about the meaning of *gossamer* since, in this sentence, it refers to a spider web.
3. Have students list possible meanings for *gossamer* in this context.
4. Look up the word and choose an appropriate meaning from the dictionary choices:
   a. filmy cobweb
   b. soft, filmy cloth
   c. lightweight waterproof cloth
5. Write the chosen meaning above the target word in the sentence to see if it carries a meaning that fits the context.

The essential point is that students must focus on the initial context of the sentence in choosing an appropriate meaning.

Using Encyclopedia Indexes

Instruction in using encyclopedias may focus initially on using the index to locate information about a topic. Students usually are surprised that encyclopedia indexes are found in a separate volume and are subdivided elaborately. The cross-referencing and page references take some explaining before students can use them independently. Before students look at an actual encyclopedia index, have students think about a topic—usually a country serves as a good example—and list possible subtopics to learn about. Items such as location, industries, transportation, and cities may be mentioned. Explain that encyclopedias subdivide topics and provide page locations where each can be found. Let each student develop his own topic for inquiry and write it as a question. This time, the topic may refer to whatever the student wishes to explore. Students also need to list possible subtopics that interest them. A student's preliminary notes might look like the following:

> *Are gorillas bigger than people?*
>
> Size
> Places where you find them
>   zoos
>   jungles
> Capturing
> Food for gorillas

Once these preliminaries are complete, students are ready to take a turn at looking in the encyclopedia index for information.

▶ **suggested activities**

WRITING REPORTS FROM ENCYCLOPEDIAS.   Instruct students to read an encyclopedia entry with their own purpose clearly in mind. Once they locate the appropriate article, they may need to skim to find the section of the write-up that answers their particular questions. The appropriate section needs to be read the first time through simply to understand its information. During the second reading, students jot down major headings and list significant subpoints. The idea is to concentrate on information in the article and write only single words or phrases that help in remembering its information.

With the encyclopedia pushed aside or closed completely, the student then uses his notes to put the information into his own words. His task is to answer the question he started with and include points mentioned in his notes. The encyclopedia can be used to check information but not to provide the wording for the report. When the first draft is complete, the student should reread his work and fix needed sentences, spellings, and punctuation.

GROUP REPORTS.   This activity works well with social studies or science units where students are investigating an unknown person or topic. Divide the class into groups of four. Each group chooses a report topic drawn from the unit of study and examines it to identify four specific, related areas or subtopics to be investigated, one by each member of the group. These might include historical background, main contribution or importance, relevance to the unit, and relevance to the students' lives. Each member of the group chooses an area and investigates the topic with that specific focus in mind. The students collaborate on their findings and share ideas. After they finish their research, each student puts his findings in writing and submits them to the other group members. The group decides if the findings fulfill the initial research purpose and if the writing is clear. They then decide if there are other questions needing to be answered. If necessary, the group conducts further research and meets again to review the new work. Once the group is satisfied with the findings, the members work together to synthesize the information into a report that is presented to the entire class. Final reports may take any number of forms (plays, stories, or traditional oral reading).

NEWSLETTER TO PARENTS.   This activity not only provides information to parents but also reinforces content area learning. Students are divided into groups of four and each group is assigned an area of current study in the classroom. The group collaborates and writes an account of current topics, why they are important to students, and what activities are involved. After writing, the groups exchange compositions and offer suggestions. The review group may raise questions and comment on the clarity and completeness of the writing, but not on its form. Once the compositions have been returned, the group then reviews the suggestions and comments and expands or revises the writing if necessary. The final revised writings are compiled, copied, and sent home to parents as a newsletter.

DICTIONARY STUDY: FINDING A WORD YOU CANNOT SPELL.   Students often complain that they cannot find a particular word in the dictionary because they do not know how to spell it. They regard the possibility of looking in the wrong place or of not knowing where to look as a formidable obstacle. An alternative perspective is that the student already knows how to spell most of the word, as there are just a few letters that are in question. With this perspective well in mind, students may find the following write-and-search lesson useful:

Instruction	*Example*
1. Write down your best guess for spelling the word.	govermentil
2. Think about the word to see if it is related to any word you already know.	govern
3. Add or change any letters in your guess based on your response in number 2.	governmentil
4. Underline the letters that you are unsure of in the word.	government<u>i</u>l

5. Look up the word in the dictionary,   governmental
   realizing that you may have to look up
   more than one possible spelling.

USING REFERENCE BOOKS: GUINNESS GUESS.   Perhaps the most
exciting reference book for elementary school children is the *Guinness Book of World Records*. It contains facts and pictures that rarely
fail to amaze and fascinate the reader. To use this book in an interest center, start by providing four or five copies of the book
and include a stack of 3 x 5 cards for student writing. Questions
to stimulate initial exploration can be posted to start off the activity:

Who has the world's longest fingernails?
How large was the world's biggest hamburger?

Students may use the interest center by looking up one of the
posted questions and writing a summary of the unusual facts.
They also can look through the book and write more questions
for other students to answer.

The idea of the center is to use the *Guinness Book of World
Records* as a resource for exploration and communication. The
written question-and-answer format provides an easy activity in
which reading and writing are integrated. It also gives students
an opportunity to write for a new audience—other students.

SUGGESTED READINGS

Askov, E. M. and K. Kamm. *Study Skills in the Content Areas*. Boston: Allyn and
   Bacon, 1982.
Haley-James, Shirley. "Helping Students Learn Through Writing." *Language Arts*
   59, no. 7 (October 1982): 726–31.
Johnson, Eric W. "Making the Most of Classroom Discussions." *Learning* 10, no.
   2 (September 1981): 125–30.
Smith, Carl and Sharon Smith. "Study Skills in Content Areas." In P. Lamb and
   R. Arnold (eds.), *Teaching Reading*. Belmont, Calif.: Wadsworth Publishing,
   1980.
Tutolo, D. J. "The Study Guide—Types, Purposes, and Value." *Journal of Reading*
   20 (March 1977): 503–07.
Wood, Karen D. and John A. Mateja. "Adapting Secondary Level Strategies for
   Use in Elementary Classrooms." *The Reading Teacher* 36, no. 6 (February
   1983): 492–97.

Chapter 9

TEACHING WRITTEN COMPOSITION

ELEMENTS IN TEACHING WRITTEN COMPOSITION

Whether a teacher starts from the premise that written composition should be free and unstructured or should be carefully molded into a specific product, certain fundamental elements guide the teaching of composition. They are:

1. Writing builds on the child's broader sense of language communication.
2. Written composition and its conventions must be learned (taught).
3. The purpose for communicating leads to the written form it assumes.
4. A sense of audience gives life to writing.
5. Personal and cultural demands prompt the student to improve.

From an analysis of these elements, a teacher can develop an instructional plan for teaching composition. The following is a brief examination of each of these elements.

1. Written communication is seen conceptually by the child as an extension of other communication, especially spoken messages. The young child probably expects words and ideas to flow onto paper as easily as they come from the mouth. Only with more and more exposure to professional writing will that concept be altered. Initially it is quite acceptable to encourage children to

use their existing oral language and their spontaneous thoughts to form the basis of their written communications. Even though written communication eventually becomes different from "talk written down," children can be put at ease by thinking they can use in writing the same style and expression that they use when speaking.

2. Written communication is different from oral communication. Written communication uses signals (conventions) to delineate ideas, as with paragraphs and sentences, and to indicate some of the ways a person uses his voice, as with commas for pauses and question marks for a question inflection. These conventions and many others are usually learned gradually over years of instruction.

3. There are many forms a written composition may assume (narrative, argument, letter), and the choice of form is guided by the purpose of the communication. Throughout the elementary curriculum children can be shown samples of the alternatives and given practice in selecting a form based on their purpose for communicating. Short stories, friendly letters, and other simple forms should be introduced first to accommodate the purposes and stage of development of young children.

4. A sense of audience gives life and effectiveness to a communication. It usually takes a few years for children to understand how to shift language and examples as they try to appeal to a different audience. Reviewing written samples or models can help students form that sense, as can writing while holding in mind the image of a person who represents the audience being addressed. As with other complex issues, this sense of audience evolves with instruction and maturation.

5. Improvement in communication most often stems from a perceived need. Children can often gain approval from parents, grandparents, or friends for their ability to express themselves. The older they get, the more important peer recognition and approval become. The school, however, sets the climate for that approval. If the school's priorities place high emphasis on sports, social events, and scores on standardized tests, then peer approval will also focus on those priorities. If communication, especially written communication, is a priority for the school staff, then displays, awards, readings, and public acknowledgment for composition must be given the time and rewards that any top priority

deserves. It is futile to bemoan our students' ineffectiveness when it is clear to them and the world that their teachers do not place any significant value on written composition.

▶ **ideas for student discussion and interaction**

Help students appreciate the similarities and the differences between speech communication and written communication. Written composition is concerned with delivering ideas through words and the conventions of written English. Communicating through speech has significant differences from communicating in writing. Cues from body language, false starts on sentences with subsequent restating of sentences, and the characteristic arm and hand gestures that make speech communication an understandable vehicle for most people are elements not available in written communication. The intended message may be the same, and words are certainly the primary vehicles for both, but written communication requires a host of different learning skills that must be added to the students' resources. Spelling, marking pauses and inflections, sentence formation, capitalization, an economy of words, and organization are a few of the skills needed for writing that are not demanded for speaking. An occasional discussion of these differences should help students maintain a perspective helpful for learning to communicate in writing.

▶ **suggested activities**

BUILDING ON ORAL READING.   In learning to write, students gain an important psychological advantage in knowing that they are using the same language that is already an automatic part of their communication capability. For example, when young children dictate stories that others write down for them, they begin to see a primitive relationship between composing orally and composing in writing.

To help students visualize the relationship between writing and other forms of language, have individuals read aloud while others describe what the voice does at the marks in the text (pauses at commas, falling voice at periods, rising voice at question marks, emphasis on important words, and so on). The students will not put all those sight/sound relationships into practice immediately, but gradually they become conscious that their books and their speech can in fact serve as guides to their writing.

LEARNING THE CONVENTIONS OF WRITING.   Refined written composition evolves over many years of practice and through the desire to communicate well. A student learns, for example, that a sentence begins with a capital letter and ends with a period. He or she then writes a letter to grandma, displaying the first semblances of marked-off sentences. To give this kind of learning a more solid base, teachers should design the writing tasks close to the students' lives. Writing letters to friends or relatives, writing stories for younger children, or describing a school event for parents are tasks that prompt students to examine their practice exercises more carefully and to seek out the conventions of writing that help them communicate effectively. Older children could write a paper for one of their age-mates, asking that person to retell what they have read. That kind of feedback helps emphasize the value of a precise use of vocabulary and common conventions.

ESTABLISHING A PURPOSE.   Composition assignments ordinarily examine the students' ability to communicate their experience in some defined way. Can they write letters? Can they describe an event or a process? Can they explain or defend an issue? For that reason, elementary school students are usually asked to write about their own experience.

The experience may be personal (I saw a freak automobile wreck) or the result of reading (An archaeologist discovers a new site for exploration). The purpose of the writing exercise may be free and open (Write your experience in any way that seems good to you) or it may be structured to a specific purpose (Let's see if you can write a short story about building a paper mill in the Amazon jungle). By alternating between those two general purposes, students can experience the psychological lift of making their own choice of purpose and form as well as produce according to defined standards. The sense of purpose is one of the most powerful aids to clear, valuable writing.

AUDIENCE OF ONE.   The language and the content of writing change according to the audience. Help students visualize their audience by writing to someone very specific, for example, the principal, the janitor, or the child in the next seat. Alternatively, have the children bring in a picture of a relative or friend, or a picture of a group, such as a football team, and place it on their desks as they write a letter to the person(s) in the picture. A picture helps keep a vivid sense of audience in the student's mind.

MOTIVATION FOR IMPROVEMENT.   Often children will want to improve because their peers exert an unseen social pressure. As long as communication is emphasized, numerous opportunities to share compositions within the class will arise. As the teacher discusses writing with an individual or with the entire class, he or she can say, "Let's see how we can say that better. Let's see how we can improve what is being communicated." In that way, a sample sentence written on the chalkboard from someone's paper or a paragraph shown on an overhead transparency gently reminds everyone that their classmates can help them. They are more likely to pay attention to punctuation or figures of speech if they know that their classmates will be suggesting improvements for their paper, even though the owner of the paper has not been identified by name.

A BASIC STRATEGY FOR TEACHING COMPOSITION

We are always searching for simple answers to complex questions, such as, How does one teach children to read? Of course, there is no easy answer to this because children and learning are complicated matters. That does not mean that individual teachers may not work from a basic strategy. Inherent in successful teaching is a sense of goals and how to achieve them (Rosenshine, 1976). In that sense, composition is no different from any other aspect of the elementary school curriculum.

Many writing teachers now use a description of the writing process that can guide them as a basic strategy. Writing can be viewed as a three-stage process: (1) predrafting or time spent in focusing, collecting, and organizing; (2) writing, or drafting the message; and (3) revising and making the message presentable to an audience. By recognizing these stages, teachers can plan activities to promote student effort at each stage. Class time must be assigned to each one regularly in order for students to gain a sense of how the process works.

▶ ideas for student discussion and interaction

To give students a sense of the three stages of the writing process, a teacher may want to demonstrate how he or she personally writes a story or an explanation. By using the chalkboard, books, and chart paper, the teacher could proceed through the stages of getting ready, drafting the message, and then revising it to make it more effective, even if it is only a short letter to be sent home to the students' parents.

Students in the class could be invited to describe how they develop a written message. Questions and comments would help raise their awareness of the three stages.

▶ suggested activities

If the writing process can be viewed at three distinctive stages, student learning may be improved by giving them time and special learning activities related to each of the three stages: predrafting, drafting, and revising. Predrafting allows time for collecting and organizing ideas. Drafting is the stage of trying to put connected ideas on paper. Revising is clarifying ideas and making the communication presentable for an audience.

PREDRAFTING: DESCRIBE AN EVENT FOR A FRIEND.   Students first need to choose their audience—a friend, a cousin, or whomever. Then, keeping the friend in mind, they should identify an event, picture it in their mind, rehearse the sequence, list a few words that capture and remind them of the event, and perhaps jot down a few notes that will guide their writing or give the description a particular slant or purpose. They should be encouraged to determine particular characteristics about their friend's background that are pertinent to describing this event. What ideas need to be included to make this event understandable to that friend? These notes can be used to discuss and to formulate their intended compositions.

WRITING-DRAFTING: LABEL AND WRITE.   Purpose and audience are as important to effective writing as they are to reading. To make those concepts practical, student writers need clear reminders of purpose and audience. Some teachers find it helpful to have students write their purpose on one 3 x 5 card and describe their audience on another card. These cards are propped up on the student's desk throughout the drafting and revision stages.

After a while, it may be just as effective to have the students state the purpose and the audience at the top of the first page of their composition, as in the following example:

Topic: Big Car Wreck

Purpose: Describe the event
Audience: Cousin Henry, who lives in the country

The message is then drafted. Students should be encouraged to erase or cross out and insert words as needed while they are drafting the message. Keep reminding them that at this point they are simply working on and shaping a draft and that they should not be worrying about producing a finished communication.

REVISING: GET A REACTION.   In view of the importance of purpose and audience, the student rereads and makes appropriate changes. A classmate can aid by responding to the questions, If you were my friend (my cousin), what would not be clear to you? and What could be changed so it reads better? At this stage it is critical that students work on ideas and clarity, not just correcting spelling and punctuation.

The student makes suggested changes and submits the paper. It always creates a better atmosphere if the revised paper can actually be submitted to the intended audience, although this is not always possible.

SEQUENCE AND DEVELOPMENT IN CHILDREN'S WRITINGS

Written composition is here defined as an understandable written message communicated through words and sentences. Children need some preliminary understandings before they can begin

writing messages. They must realize that their ideas ma
words that are represented by alphabetic symbols, and
orderly arrangement of those words is needed for a read
derstand the message. This definition does not deny the value of
very young children making squiggly marks and drawing pictures
and calling it "My Story." That early stage is certainly leading up
to written composition, just as repeating stories, listening to stories, and putting pictures in sequence comprise some background
and readiness experiences for written composition. But in a practical, pedagogical sense, written composition begins when the
child realizes that this process requires putting recognizable words
on paper and that what he writes must be interpretable.

In a developmental sequence, then, the child must be able
to write the letters of the alphabet, have a basic sense of the separation of words, and be able to order the written words in ar-
rangements that are usually sentences. Thereafter, no precise sequence of skills must be followed, but most teachers will want to
use some identified sequence for making instructional decisions.
A textbook or a curriculum guide usually provides a sequence
that can be used for guiding student growth.

▶ **ideas for student discussion and interaction**

Competence in writing evolves gradually over years of learning and practice. To help children understand their need to learn
and practice, ask them how they learn a game or sport and then
become more skilled at it. Some sample responses might be: they
watch and imitate; they get instructions and try to carry them out;
they play the game and then practice certain parts of it, as in
shooting baskets for basketball. Use this as a basis for comparing
other learning tasks, and lead them to discuss and appreciate that
composition requires the same kind of learning and practice.

▶ **suggested activities**

SELF-DIAGNOSIS.   One way to focus children's attention on
the need for growth and improvement is through self-diagnosis.
After they have drafted and revised one composition, give them
a checklist to attach to their paper. They can use the checklist as
a guide for reviewing their paper and as a record for the teacher,

Figure 9.1
Sample Growth List

Name _____ Date _____

    After revising my paper, I want to work on these areas to help me become a better writer.

SAMPLE LIST	EXAMPLES
Vocabulary	horizontal, vertical
Spelling	accommodate
Handwriting	d, g *
Using words correctly	accept, not except ✔
Punctuation	colon ✔
Capitalization	The Eagles (organizations)
Organizing ideas	compare and contrast ✔
Other	

    Put an asterisk next to the one you want to work on right away.
    Put a check mark next to the ones you want to work on this year.

---

who wants to see what needs the children are identifying. It should be reasonably simple, as in figure 9.1.

    The teacher can review these growth lists periodically to form groups for special work or to use them as a list of specifics to discuss with individuals as she responds to their papers.

    THEMES FOR DISPLAY COMPOSITIONS.   Compositions on themes or issues and compositions that represent written debates within the class make fine bulletin board and hallway displays. In addition to creating a sense of importance, displaying compositions enables students to share ideas or information and provides a forum to encourage positive constructive comments about the compositions. By having a comment sheet attached to each displayed composition, students can be encouraged to provide reactions that will help the writer. Those reactions may be either content reactions or literary comments, such as ideas for improving communication, style, and organization. Great care needs to be paid to guiding children in making constructive comments. No one should be permitted to make comments that are hurtful or vindictive.

Give students a list of phrases that lead to constructive suggestions such as:

I suggest these changes because . . . .
This section is not clear to me because . . . .
An example might help to . . . .
I did not get the point here because . . . .
I find your handwriting difficult to read because . . . .

Negative words are not permitted because they are hurtful, not helpful. This includes such words as *lousy, terrible, stinks, horrid,* and *bad*.

Try these topics as composition starters:

if I were in charge of the world (state, school, country)
my hero
if I were my father (mother, teacher)
three steps to happiness
how to drive your parents bananas
how I would save the whales (eagles, elephants)
how I like to spend my favorite holiday
getting set for a hobby
the most exciting game and how it's played
ways to get acquainted in a new crowd
how to change your personality
exploring a corner of the world (of space)
selecting a wardrobe
figuring out my ambitions
surviving school
my best school subject and why
my worst school subject and why
how to make a better me

RIDDLES AND OTHER COMPOSITION IDEAS.   Have students develop their own riddles organized around the days of the week. The designer of the riddle begins the process by giving a vague clue for the first day of the week. For example, if the answer to the riddle is "the moon," perhaps the first day's clue would be the single word "space." Any member of the class may then guess at the answer, but has only one guess for the week. Each succeeding day, a more specific clue is given (until someone guesses the correct answer), as indicated in the following example. Place the clue for each day of the week on a large calendar where classmates can view the information as it is supplied.

Clues

Sunday:	Space
Monday:	I am a large ball of rock.
Tuesday:	I give off no light of my own. My color is really dusty brown, but I look like I am a silvery color because of the sun's light.
Wednesday:	During every month I seem to change my size and shape.
Thursday:	If you visited me, you would weigh less than you do right now.
Friday:	A nursery rhyme tells of a cow jumping over me.
Saturday:	I'm the MOON.

IDEAS FOR THOSE WHO LIKE TO WRITE.   Some children like to write and need only a list of general ideas to get them started. The following list could be duplicated and taped to the inside cover of the students' books or could be made into a wall chart that hangs as a constant reminder of types of writing. Some teachers post this list and challenge their students to produce one of each type over the course of the school year. Perhaps a writers' interest group could be formed to produce and display one of these types every two weeks of the school year.

stories
editorials
letters
scripts for a play
events in poetry form
routes for a trip
assignments for a newspaper
scripts for radio or television
leaflets
biographies
limericks

speeches
notices or news items
book news sections
headlines
questions: who, what, where (closed); why in your opinion
   (open)

IDEAS FOR THOSE WHO LIKE TO MAKE THINGS.   To link composition with arts and crafts, have children become the illustrator or the builder and writer-explainer within the same project. Each art project must be accompanied by written explanations or stage directions. Another option for writing would be to have the artist try to teach or convince classmates to produce similar products. Here is a short list of arts and crafts ideas to link with writing.

animated map, relief map, outline map, class map (using
   overhead projector to show and explain the map)
bulletin board design (using overhead projector to show how
   to organize and highlight information)
models of cars, planes, and so on, as displays of personal
   hobbies
diorama, table scenes, as visualizations of events from class
   study or personal experience
fold-out chart series with drawings and descriptions to demonstrate events, how-to-do-it projects, biographical and
   historical themes
graphs and charts of science or social studies information (using overhead projector or bulletin board display)
murals for the classroom or school hallway to depict the reading interests of the children
advertisements and/or posters for school events.
book illustrations of popular or highly rated books
slide story of a field trip or other local event
stick or finger puppets
cartoons with captions

IDEAS FOR THOSE WHO LIKE SPEAKING.   Some children would benefit from linking written composition to speech activities. In this instance they prepare scripts and presentation notes as a means to deliver their programs or speeches. The script, outlines, or notes would then become an integral part of any evaluation of the presentation. Some categories that follow (for instance, debates) are not appropriate for primary-grade children, but these types of oral presentations lend themselves to a written component, whether the audience is classmates, younger children, or a gathering of parents.

radio skits
debates
plays
puppet shows
shadow plays
panel discussions
monologues
reports
thumbnail sketches of interesting people
    a. person: name, personal description, reason for importance
    b. accomplishments: list in sequence or in appropriate categories
interviews
committee work
demonstration or explanation of how to play a game or operate a machine
verbal announcements
narration of an event, for example, using a filmstrip or recounting a T.V. program
reading of excerpts from a favorite book for tape recording

Any of these could be written and then read into a tape recorder.

► **activities for the slow starter**

The following are some examples of writing activities that can be used with novice writers or with more accomplished students in need of some fresh ideas. Single words or phrases are acceptable for many of these activities since the intent is to get students used to the idea of jotting down their thoughts and feelings.

CATEGORIZING.   Supply the students with a general term or category and have them give word samples for it. For example, have the students list all the "fluffy" words they can think of such as pillow, cloud, cotton candy, and so on. Various terms can be given (loud words, sharp words), and later this can be expanded to sentence writing in which the children try to use each word in a sentence.

CLOZE TECHNIQUE.   Create a story leaving blanks in place of every fifth or eighth word. Have the students fill in the blanks as they wish. A discussion of the chosen words can emphasize the vocabulary development aspects of this exercise or the use of various clues in determining an appropriate word.

TALKING TELEGRAMS.   Slow starters need to have reality in their writing and reading. People send telegrams to congratulate, to express sympathy, and to make important announcements. Have the students write messages of 25 words or less on telegram blanks. They then read (or post) their telegram. It is helpful for all ages to try to confine a message to 25 words.

GREETING CARDS.   The students can prepare personal cards for special occasions, such as get well or birthday cards for friends and relatives. The students can then either send or deliver them. This exercise offers an opportunity to discuss the vocabulary associated with joyous occasions and with positive expressions about health. Children could collect commercial cards to compare with the ones they create.

ACROSTICS.   Use the children's names or a fanciful word of their choice to make a sentence or serve as a story starter. For example, the name *James* could be made to read:

James
Always
Makes
Excellent
Soup

This sentence could then be used as the theme of a paragraph or short story.

SECRET PALS.   Eveyone enjoys receiving letters. Letters from children in another room or, better yet, children in another school create a highly stimulating reading and writing environment. Although letters can be delivered in a bunch, primary-grade children like having their own mailbox in their room. Shoe boxes on a shelf or another simple divider technique can create a box for each child. By arranging an exchange system with one or two other teachers, a teacher can plan to have letters written and sent one week with responses received the next, alternating throughout the year.

DAILY JOURNAL.   In order to increase the volume of writing and to create a sense of comfort with writing, there is little substitute for a personal journal. The students write a personal entry daily in their journal. These writings are only for themselves, unless they choose to share them. Teachers may ask to see one entry each week, an entry chosen by the student.

COMIC STRIPS.   Prepare examples from a favorite comic strip or have the students start their own. Leave all the "bubbles" blank for the students to fill in their own story line. The comic strip is a comfortable form of writing for children in grades three and up, as they often enjoy the idea of providing the words to convey the action of the pictures.

ALLITERATIVE LETTERS.   The students make up tongue twisters that have each word beginning with the same letter (for example, Lovely little Lisa likes licking luscious lemon lollipops). Perhaps students would enjoy a class contest to see who can develop the most difficult eight-to-ten-word tongue twister. All entries could be posted for review, practice, nomination, and vote for the toughest tongue twister. This activity is especially fun for middle-grade students.

GRAB BAG GUESSING.   Put a mystery item in a bag. Have the students reach into the bag and feel the object. Then let them write a detailed description of how it felt and what it was. Use objects with distinctive shapes or textures such as a toothbrush, velvet ribbon, or a fur-lined glove. This may be adapted to activities stressing smell, sound, taste, and so on. Vocabulary development and attention to sensory details can serve as purposes for this activity.

Additional composition activities and means for evaluating compositions by students and teachers are found in chapter 10.

SUGGESTED READINGS

Dionisio, Marie. "Write? Isn't This Reading Class?" *The Reading Teacher* 36, no. 8 (April 1983): 746–50.

Esgar, L. P. "Drawing Their Own Conclusions." *The Reading Teacher* 31 (1978):444–46.

Graves, Donald H. *Writing: Teachers and Children at Work.* Exeter, N.H.: Heinemann Educational Books, 1983.

Rosenshine, Barak. "Recent Research on Teaching Behaviors and Student Achievement." *Journal of Teaching Education* 27 (Spring 1976):61–64.

Chapter 10

PROOFREADING AND REVISING

GETTING STUDENTS TO REVISE

No one minds assigning compositions; it is *correcting* them that becomes a task. For as long as anyone can remember, teachers have lamented the time-consuming problem of correcting student compositions. Various relief systems have been attempted, including hiring "paper-graders." Whatever the value of those isolated relief activities, the broad population of teachers has not benefited from outside help. What is even more disturbing is that very little evidence exists to show that the time a teacher spends in correcting themes will pay off in improved writing skill for the student.

We believe that for the sake of the teacher's time and for the benefit of improved student composition, a necessary alternative is to teach students to correct their own errors before handing in their papers. To do this, students and teachers need to develop an attitude about producing compositions. Writing a paper needs to be seen as a stage-by-stage process involving the generation of ideas, drafting a paper, and revising the paper for submission to the teacher. Proofreading, therefore, becomes an integral part of learning how to produce compositions. The result should be more capable students and less harried teachers.

Clarity of Communication

As is the case with any teaching objective, proofreading and revising do not occur through magic or prayer. The teacher has a significant role to play in promoting an attitude and in gradually leading students to self-sufficiency. The teacher starts by creating an awareness that writing is communicating. The clearer the writing, the better the communication. Sometimes that sense can be promoted by making transparencies of "anonymous" compositions and asking the students to comment on ways to make the composition more effective. Samples of compositions can also be duplicated via photocopier or ditto machine—with student names omitted—in order to give each student a personal opportunity to improve predetermined characteristics of that composition. Or, selected paragraphs could be written on the chalkboard to elicit improvements, thereby raising the group's awareness of means for clarifying and emphasizing ideas expressed in their writing.

The importance of clarity can be promoted by the teacher who refuses to accept sloppy papers or garbled prose. As a demonstration, a teacher may even want to show how she revises a personal composition, thus emphasizing the need for everyone to raise questions about his or her own writing to see if it delivers the message in an acceptable and understandable form.

With communication as the focus, the teacher points out that legibility, spelling, grammar, and accurate use of language can each in turn (and later altogether) be the target for proofreading and revision. By regularly working with sentences or paragraphs from individuals in the class, the teacher shows incidentally that attention to the conventions of writing has daily, real-life significance. By selecting one or two areas at a time (spelling, for example), the students see that the task is manageable.

After observing student samples and deciding that the class needs work in specific aspects of proofreading, the teacher may assign commercial practice materials to clarify and to refine through repetitive exercises on specific grammar, spelling, or organizational skills. By that time, students should have the perspective of seeing how the practice exercises will benefit them in their future writing. Even though no names are used when student compositions are presented for class analysis, the process makes students conscious of the social aspects of their writing. By having peer teams evaluate and work with one another in revising compositions, a teacher can promote the positive social pressure for better compositions.

The intent of the following exercises is to show how students can be led to think for themselves about their own writing. As students become able to criticize their own work, teachers can devote more time and energy to substantive and organizational issues in the compositions. In other words, teachers can pay attention to an evaluation of the whole composition and leave many proofreading and revision activities to the students.

PROOFREADING STRATEGY

The Teacher's Role

The teacher is concerned with making proofreading practice a learning experience for the students. Neither the students nor the teacher should think that it is the teacher's job alone to review each paper to see how to improve it. But as long as the teacher persists in marking each paper with great precision, the students will take a minimum amount of interest in their own proofreading habits. The teacher's role, then, is to develop a consciousness in the students and to help students learn the rules and guidelines that will assist them in constructing papers that are legible, well organized, and spelled correctly. The teacher's first responsibility is to see that the students are actively engaged in proofreading. That would suggest the submission of a draft with notations on it to indicate that the student proofread his or her own paper.

The Draft and Review Technique

The following technique for proofreading and review requires the active participation of the student in improving the quality of his or her writing. The first step is to have the student write a double-spaced draft. Instead of erasing, the student circles those words or sections intended for correction, and writes her suggested changes in the space above the circled words.

Once the student has finished this review, the first draft with notations is submitted to the teacher. The teacher does not correct the paper but only makes one of two marks at the top: *OK* or *P*. *OK* means that in a cursory review the teacher sees that the proofreading process is at work and he does not notice any evident errors or problems. The student may then rewrite and submit a cleaned-up version. A mark of *P* with a *1, 2, 3,* or *4* indicates that the teacher has noticed a problem or error. The student must do further proofreading and then show the teacher that changes have been made. The numbers *1, 2, 3,* and *4* represent the quarter of the page or paragraph where the teacher noticed the problem. (It is important to recall that the purpose of teacher review is to encourage progress and not to guarantee a perfect paper.) There is nothing to prevent the teacher from noticing errors in all quarters of the paper—provided the teacher wants the student to carry out an extensive review.

Those papers marked with a *P* must be resubmitted to demonstrate that the student has made additional corrections (progress). After a resubmission, the teacher may then return the papers with an *OK* to write the final draft. That draft can then be graded or used for display as the occasion demands.

Choose a Proofreading Focus

The above technique reflects an attitude about the purpose of school writing and the part that proofreading plays. Papers are submitted to encourage progress. Proofreading could alternately focus on spelling, grammar, organization, legibility, or something as esoteric as using metaphors consistently. Have the class choose one focus and discuss what it entails. In all these areas, however, the teacher helps the student become conscious of his or her own need to proofread, that is, the need to become a more effective communicator. Thus the teacher and the student share the responsibility of learning how to improve.

GROUP APPROACH TO PROOFREADING

Student Responsibility

Students can be asked to correct their own papers from the first day a composition is requested. The secret is to ask for only one thing at a time. Asking students to proofread their papers and remove "all errors" seems overwhelming at the beginning. By having them work in small groups looking for a specific kind of improvement, they will usually teach each other.

Team Correction

The teams may be two, three, or four students working together. They exchange their papers and make notations according to the directions of the teacher.

The teacher begins by explaining the topic or target for improvement, which is some aspect of spelling, grammar, organization, paragraph development, and so on. With that knowledge in mind, the students write compositions and then work in teams to revise each others' papers. *To revise* here means to help produce a better product.

Suppose the teacher wanted the students to improve their writing by using examples after general statements. She could write on the board: "All the kids in Sherwood Forest School wanted to be good students."

What does that statement mean? The teacher can show how to use a few examples or clarifying instances to make that statement more understandable, for example:

1. They wanted good citizenship certificates, which are awarded each spring.
2. They were willing to work for A and B grades.
3. They wanted parents and teachers to praise their work on assignments.

The teacher can then ask the editorial teams to see if their papers have unclear statements that could be improved by adding examples. When these teams run into questions or internal disagreements, the teacher should intervene as a roving advisor.

Before submitting a draft to the editorial team, each student reviews her own paper using the same guidelines to be observed by the team. By circling trouble spots and inserting different copy the individual student shows everyone that she is assuming personal responsibility for learning and for the drafted ideas. This individual effort should improve the efficiency of the editorial team, which can direct its attention to other areas of the composition. Individuals and the team should use a consistent marking system, such as circling the trouble spots and inserting changes, to make it easier for all concerned to locate the revision targets and the resulting changes. Using an additional diagnostic technique, some teachers ask individuals to use a lead pencil and the group to use colored pencils or a ballpoint pen to mark the paper. One major goal, of course, is to increase the perceptiveness of the individual student.

A reminder: the search for improvement has to be limited in its scope. No one, including the teacher, searches for everything. For example, search only for spelling or only for improved grammar—whatever the topic of the exercise.

Similarly, when the teacher gets the papers, he reads only for one kind of improvement, the one that is under scrutiny. When additional problems or errors are found, no notation is made. Those papers are then returned to the team for examination, discussion, and change.

▶ **ideas for student discussion and interaction**

We want students to understand that we revise our writing and thoughts not only for personal satisfaction but also for the benefit of those who read or listen to our ideas. That is one beneficial reason for working together to revise each other's papers. Discuss those ideas with students and pose questions, such as the following:

- How do the various talents of a team contribute to proofreading each other's papers?
- Would assigning one grade for proofreading to the entire team contribute benefits to the activity?

Grading on an error-reduction basis, a teacher can assign a single grade to each member of the proofreading team. Each team tries to submit papers that have as few errors as possible (that is, as few errors after team correction as possible). The teacher may give each group a grade on *their self-correcting efforts* based upon their ability to constantly reduce errors. Thus, if their first papers have a combined total of five errors, then on the next composition they must reduce the number of team errors in order to improve their grade. This technique is particularly applicable to such problems as spelling and grammatical errors.

▶ **suggested activities**

HETEROGENEOUS TEAMWORK.   It is often advantageous to
have a heterogeneous group for team proofreading. The teacher
can first divide the class into three general groups for assignment
to these teams. These three general groups are low, average, and
high performers on the skills being taught. Each proofreading team
would be composed of one person from each of the groups. That
arrangement enables an exchange of ideas among the students
and promotes a sense of responsibility across different ability levels. Besides, it takes away the inclination of all the good students
and all the poor students to get together. Each group could receive
a common grade for its self-correction work, as described above.
A separate individual grade may be assigned to the compositions
for their content and originality.

INDIVIDUAL SELF-CORRECTION.   Alternate team correction
with self-correction; sometimes individuals work entirely alone,
other times with their group. Once students understand how to
review their compositions as a result of reviewing papers in teams,
they can be asked to self-correct only (see the activity on team
correction). At first, independent self-correction should occur only
now and then, possibly every third or fourth composition. Gradually, across a semester, the burden is shifted more and more to
the individual.
   Caution! Perfection on each paper is not the purpose of the
self-correction process. The purpose is to have the student learn
the process and develop the habit of self-correction—to learn how
to proofread independently. "Improvement" is the banner word
that guides and motivates students and teacher.

ERROR-REDUCTION TECHNIQUE.   As with the team-corrected
papers, the individual proofreads his or her own paper, circling
problems and marking improvements or corrections. The self-cor-
rected papers are reviewed by the teacher and are given a notation
to indicate what the teacher's quick review revealed. Notations
in the margin show the student the approximate location of the
problems and the number of items the teacher identified for additional self-correction. The student must then circle the problem
and write in the change for a cursory review by the teacher.

Figure 10.1
Sample Error-Reduction Chart—Proofreading

Student's Name _____

DATE	TYPE OF ERROR	NUMBER OF ERRORS CORRECTED BY		COMMENTS
		STUDENT	TEACHER	
9–16	spelling	6	8	Carelessness
9–18	grammar	2	3	Verb-subject agreement
9–24	spelling	1	1	
	grammar	0	1	

For certain kinds of work, spelling for instance, each student could keep an error-reduction chart such as figure 10.1. An error-reduction chart could be kept either by the student or by the teacher, depending on its purpose. Each composition is listed by date along with the type of proofreading to be carried out. The listing of the number of errors may be done once for each composition to indicate all the errors corrected by the student, or twice, the first number showing the errors the student identified and the second number including the errors added after the teacher reviewed the paper.

Finally, there is the comments section, a space for the student to remind herself of some generalization or for the teacher to give a word of advice. In spelling errors, for example, the teacher may want to remind the student that she is not taking advantage of certain spelling patterns in trying to spell some of the words. The comment section may also be used as a means for encouraging the student—"You've already cut the errors by 50 percent. That's an excellent effort."

INCREASING COMPLEXITY.   As the self-correction process becomes more habitual, the teacher will naturally want the students to review their compositions for more than a single area, such as spelling. As the process becomes familiar and as more of the elements of composition are taught and practiced in class, the students are told to expand the number of items for which they are proofreading—spelling, grammar, usage, figures of speech, paragraphing, organization, legibility, and so on. The end result should be a proofreading of the whole work. It must be restated, however, that students need to be taught to work on each single, simple element prior to proofreading for a conglomeration of skills.

In a program that emphasizes communication, that is, sharing ideas through written composition, the following proofreading priorities could be followed. The most needed areas are in the first column.

First	Second	Third
legibility	usage	organization
sensibility	end punctuation	paragraphing
coherence	vocabulary	figurative language
spelling	accuracy	

TEACHING FROM STUDENT COMPOSITIONS

Numerous studies have demonstrated that isolated practice in finding the correct word in wordbook exercises does not improve compositions—even in the areas that have been practiced. What does facilitate improvement, we believe, is the actual writing of compositions and then showing where specific skills fit into the compositions. When a student's own composition is used to illustrate how various skills appear, then learning and practicing an individual skill seem more valuable to the student. To interest the student in the improvement of writing (and speaking), we should start with something the student has written (or said). By combining a personal composition with the reactions of a peer audience, interest in and attention to revising will be developed.

Analyzing Sentences from Student Compositions

Any student language product, however meager, can be the subject for class analysis: *How can this be improved?* The class appreciates the reality once the teacher says, "This sentence (this word, this paragraph) was taken from one of your papers. Let's examine it to see how to improve it." Proceed as follows:

1. First the teacher decides what skill or principle he wants to emphasize. (It may be the one emphasized in the next chapter

of the grammar book.) He requests the class to write a composition (or paragraph) that will offer opportunities for that skill to appear. For example, where quotation marks are under scrutiny, ask the students to write a brief dialogue about such topics as school spirit, the basketball game, or an approaching holiday.

2. Using an overhead projection transparency or the chalkboard, the teacher writes sentences (examples) that are in great need of improvement. No individual student is identified, but the authors of the passages naturally know which examples are theirs. Their attention and interest are especially high.

3. The teacher then asks the class to help diagnose and correct the problems. Questions such as the following are useful: Who can find words that are misspelled? How would you improve the grammar of this sentence? Could you improve the figure(s) of speech in this paragraph?

4. Volunteers are then invited to the chalkboard or to the overhead projector to circle what they think needs improvement and to write a replacement. The group confirms the improvement or suggests something better.

5. The nature of the corrections may then be discussed and assigned for practice—perhaps through a textbook or workbook. In the case of spelling, the correctly spelled words could be listed on the board and included in the weekly spelling test, if one exists.

Quizzes from Student Papers

Previously reviewed writing samples can be used as material for a quiz on sentence correction. This would demonstrate to the students that they are learning through their own writing. The teacher selects for the quiz some of the sentences or paragraphs that have appeared on the board in their uncorrected forms. The students then correct them. It is agreed that only the corrections that occurred in the class discussion are to be included in the quiz score. If students proofread papers in small groups, each group could submit a sentence or two (and the corrections). The combined sentences then constitute the proofreading quiz. A spelling quiz could also be constructed from group proofreading. As the misspelled words are identified and then corrected, they could be listed on the chalkboard as part of the spelling list for that week.

A TEACHER NOTATION SYSTEM

Alerting Students to Problem Areas

Even after the student claims that she has proofread and corrected a paper, the teacher may still want to review the paper for mechanical errors and return it for additional work before evaluating it for its organization and content.

Upon noticing an uncorrected error, the teacher can place an *R* for "review" at the top of the page (or in the margin close to the location of the error) and return it to the student. When the student returns the paper showing that additional proofreading has been accomplished, the teacher may then evaluate it for content. Some teachers then give an *A, B, C* grade; some place an *S* on it for satisfactory; or others draw a smiling face on the paper with a brief comment, for example, "Thank you for improving your vocabulary."

A teacher can expand her proofreading notation system to suit student needs. For example:

RS = review spelling
RP = review punctuation
RG = review grammar
RH = review handwriting

This notation system can be expanded and could be posted on a wall chart or duplicated for each student. The purpose of the notation system is to emphasize the student's responsibility for proofreading. It is not meant to replace more lengthy analytic comments by the teacher.

▶ **ideas for student discussion and interaction**

Whatever techniques and notation systems a teacher uses to interest students, they can be listed on the chalkboard and students can discuss:

- Which are the most helpful?
- Which ones are not clear?

- If you could develop your own notations, what would they be?
- Can you work out a technique that would make proofreading more interesting?
- What steps do you follow when an RG or RP appears on your paper?

▶ **suggested activities**

CLEAN AND DIRTY PAPERS.   In some instances the teacher may want the students to show that they have engaged in a proofreading effort. At other times, a paper should be rewritten because it is going to be evaluated holistically by the teacher or by a panel from the class. For that purpose it should be free of circles and rewritten phrases. A paper may need to be rewritten several times because it is to be submitted for competition or because it will be put on public display. The teacher and the students have to clarify what will happen to a composition and then they can decide into which category it fits:

1. A paper that shows the scars of a proofreading procedure (the original draft may suffice).
2. A paper to be submitted to the teacher for a grade or an evaluation.
3. A paper to be placed on public display. (This category often requires the proofreading efforts of the student and the teacher and will probably be rewritten at least twice.) Knowing that a paper will be displayed is probably the most powerful motivation a student has for editing.

DEVELOPING A SPELLING CONSCIOUSNESS

Proofreading for Spelling

When a paper is submitted for a grade or presented for display, the writer does not want to be embarrassed by spelling errors. But the problem is getting students to develop a sense for accurate spelling, a kind of spelling consciousness that will alert them to possible errors and give them ways of checking those suspicious-looking words. A good speller makes use of visual memory and sound-spelling patterns, that is, auditory-visual associations. The teacher can help by encouraging students to make hypotheses about how words are spelled and by checking those hypotheses. She can also help by making sure there is a strong spelling curriculum in the school.

▶ **ideas for student discussion and interaction**

There are a number of spelling patterns that have sufficient regularity to be used as guidelines (generalizations) to help a person proofread for spelling. It would seem, however, that most people learn to spell accurately by becoming conscious of their need to do so and by developing their own techniques for handling the problems that exist in English spelling.

One way to encourage the development of personal techniques is to suggest that students keep a "spelling brain" notebook. Its purpose and contents include two things:

1. Personal techniques for remembering troublesome words, for example, the double s in *issue* (Is Sue in issue?)
2. A list of words for which the student wants to work out techniques for remembering

Each time there is a proofreading activity, students could add a "spelling brain" technique to their notebook. The techniques could be shared occasionally with a "spelling brain bulletin" or by having small groups select the three best techniques from the group and share them with the class. As a weekly five- or ten-minute exercise, it reminds students that there are interesting ways to play with words and that they have to take an active role in remembering troublesome words. The notebook should have a table of contents for easy reference.

▶ **suggested activity**

Writers, whether students or others, are trying to communicate a message. Anything that interferes with that message prevents the writer from achieving his goal. Whether those interferences are caused by poor handwriting, unintelligible language or grammar, or spelling errors, the effect is similar: the reader is distracted or focuses attention on the error rather than the message.

REVISING SPELLING FOR A DISPLAY PAPER.   Students can be helped to appreciate the communication value of spelling through papers that are put on display.

When a teacher announces that the next paper to be handed in will be displayed, the class should begin a proofreading procedure.

To prepare for a display paper, the teacher may nominate spelling as the only focus for proofreading. Partners in the class may exchange papers and help each other review for spelling errors and help find the correct spelling. It is understood that when the paper is revised and submitted the teacher will post it on the board for general reading.

All students in the class are encouraged to read the posted papers. If they note a misspelled word on the paper, they may list that word on a comment sheet that is tacked beneath each paper. When a student gets his paper back, he can circle the words that have been identified as misspelled and rewrite them correctly.

Not all errors will be found through this casual reading procedure. That is not its purpose. The purpose is to make students conscious that their spelling errors are observed by others and that errors become distractions from the message of their paper.

The teacher must caution the students to approach this display paper reading in a sense of mutual help and not one in which one student tries to belittle or intimidate another.

MAKING STUDENTS CONSCIOUS OF CAPITALIZATION AND PUNCTUATION

Besides beginning sentence capitals and ending punctuation, students do not often see the value of paying heed to capitalization and punctuation. One way to demonstrate the value of those conventions is to show on an overhead projection or on a handout a passage that ignores all conventional marks. A sample follows.

a group of scandanavians none of whom could speak english came across the u s through the great lakes to set up their community in bismarck north dakota when they arrived after many hardships mr olson a tough old sour character built a general store fancy that but he was just what the danes and swedes needed would you believe it was also a saloon

Because there are appositives, exclamations, and questions in that passage, it takes considerable work to determine the nuances of the message in its present condition. Such an example enables the teacher to demonstrate the need for marks that signal different structures and inflections.

▶ ideas for student discussion and interaction

The same unmarked passage can be used to stimulate student discussion and attitude about capitalization and punctuation. Ask questions like these:

- What do capitalization and punctuation do for the reader?
- Why should a writer spend time working on punctuation? Capitalization?
- Where can you find the answers you need about what to capitalize and punctuate?

▶ suggested activity

SHARE A COMMA.   Direct students to write a paragraph (message) without any capitalization or punctuation. Then they exchange papers with a neighbor, and each tries to place marks and capitals where they belong. They discuss what they have done and try to work out disagreements. Those matters that they cannot decide are brought up later before the entire class for general discussion.

When a question is raised before the entire group, write the sentence on the board so the entire class can see the problem in its concrete form. Wherever possible have other students give the correct answer to a question raised.

For a variation of this exercise, have the students place their papers in a box. Each student draws a paper, corrects it, and signs it. The papers are then returned to the teacher for review.

The teacher can specify a minimum number of capital letters or punctuation marks that the originator of the message must include, such as at least six of each. The class can also be divided into groups, with each group assigned a specific type of punctuation or capitalization problem to include in their papers, such as words in a series, names of organizations, exclamations, or questions. The students then write their individual messages and exchange them as described above.

LEGIBILITY AND HANDWRITING STYLE

Helping Students to Write Legibly

Handwriting has many personal characteristics, for example, size, slant, regularity of form, neatness or sense of control, and so on. Despite these differences, no reader should have to struggle unduly to read a communication that is sent out. Being legible in personal letters and in class exercises is a matter of courtesy. The teacher can help students understand that while personal handwriting styles can vary considerably, there is still a need for the courtesy of legibility.

Acceptability depends on purpose. If a person is making notes for himself, then he can be as lax and brief and sloppy with his handwriting as he wishes—just as long as he can read his own message. But once the paper is meant to be distributed to someone else, legibility is a definite consideration. Illegible handwriting places a burden on the reader, one he should not have to bear.

Group Criteria

To help students appreciate legibility, show them that the standards vary depending on who is to read the paper. Divide them into groups of six or eight and have each student submit any written paper from any class. As the papers are passed around, each person should circle any word that he finds difficult to decipher because of legibility problems—inadequate distinctiveness of letters, letters run together, sloppiness, or whatever.

When all papers have been reviewed, the group should examine the differences that exist. Some papers will have relatively few circles on them and some will have many. The group should evaluate each paper to see under which condition it might be acceptable. Some might be acceptable as personal drafts meant to be read by the writer only; some might be acceptable as working copies, that is, copies that could be shared with a classmate for reviewing and getting help; and some might be acceptable as display copies or copies to be turned in for a final grade or displayed on a bulletin board. Given those three choices, ask students to label each of the papers that they have.

As part of this exercise, the teacher reminds them that this is an attempt to make them conscious of the variation in handwriting and how handwriting may differ depending on the person or persons to whom the message will be communicated.

It is also important at this time for the teacher to indicate any *personal standards* he has for papers to be submitted for a grade. Those standards should be identified in a concrete way, probably by using samples of student papers that are acceptable and not acceptable. Those samples could be posted, duplicated and distributed, or shown on overhead projection transparencies with caution taken to keep the authors anonymous. Students should understand that the teacher has the right to reject any paper that is very difficult to read. This approach does not value handwriting over content; it values communication, and legibility as a necessary component. Once these standards have been established, the teacher should return those papers that do not meet minimum standards for legibility—no matter in which subject they are submitted.

▶ **suggested activities**

LEGIBILITY CHECKLIST.   For a gradual introduction to comparative handwriting, it is helpful for the teacher first to show samples on the overhead projector asking for comments from the students on what makes one sample of handwriting easier to read than another. Then the teacher can pass out a checklist similar to the one shown in figure 10.2 and divide the class into small groups asking them to share samples of their own handwriting for an analysis against the checklist. Each member of the team rates each

Figure 10.2
Legibility Checklist

	YES	NO
1. Are open letters readily distinguished from closed letters? For example: e-i, l-t, cl-d	____	____
2. Are r, m, n, u, v, w clearly distinguishable?	____	____
3. Do the tall letters consistently stand out above the short letters?	____	____
4. Are a-e, g-q-p, h-k clearly distinguishable?	____	____
5. Is there an adequate space between words?	____	____
6. Is it easy to see where one sentence ends and the next begins?	____	____
7. Overall, is the writing easy to read?	____	____

handwriting sample of approximately 100 words against the checklist and attaches his rating to that sample. When each one has evaluated all the samples, the group discusses the merits of each sample and identifies what contributes to the legibility of that sample. If this exercise is done from time to time, it will enable students to keep legibility in mind as they write.

SELF-CHECK.   As a follow-up activity, the teacher should ask students to use the same checklist to evaluate samples of their own writing and to then rewrite the first 100 words trying to incorporate improvements that they deem necessary. This type of evaluation should be done after a composition has been written in the normal fashion.

Everyone's handwriting has its own distinctive features and the purpose of any handwriting exercise is to increase legibility, not to create uniformity. The teacher can promote legibility not only with exercises similar to those described above but also by returning papers that are difficult to read or done in a sloppy manner. However, guidelines for making rejected papers legible should accompany their return, guidelines such as those discussed in figure 10.2.

THE GRAPHOLOGIST.   One way to help students understand the value of their personal handwriting styles and legibility is to approach it from the point of view of the graphologist, someone who studies handwriting. Assign several students to get some easy-to-read books on graphology and prepare a class presentation on what they learn. By taking sample papers from the class (papers that are prepared for normal submission in the class) and providing a brief analysis of each one, the student graphologists can focus attention on handwriting and its significance. The comments of the student graphologists should not dwell on the personality traits that may be identified through such analysis, but should be primarily concerned with topics such as the slant, legibility, and idiosyncrasies that show up in the handwriting. Discussing these points will call attention to what handwriting reveals about the person.

FIRST APPEARANCES.   Along with a discussion of handwriting, it may be helpful to show how legibility affects grades. Show a few sample papers to the class and ask them to make a judgment from their first impression, that is, their attitude based upon neatness and legibility, about the quality of the work. Their answers may reveal how an initial impression colors a person's judgment. They will probably have positive reactions toward those papers that are clear and neat and negative reactions toward those that are not. Teachers have the same reactions. In a circumstance where subjective factors enter into the grading of a paper, such as an English composition or an essay in social studies, the grade of the sloppy and barely legible paper is going to suffer (even though the content may be quite good).

SAMPLES FROM OTHER GRADES.   It might be worth showing that handwriting is developmental by picking up samples from other teachers across the grades. In the primary grades when children are first learning to write, their handwriting tends to be more uniform and has fewer distinctive characteristics than years later when a person has developed a personal cursive handwriting style. Those developmental stages are normal and the point is to make sure that any style that is developed is readable, that there is separation between words and letters, and that the letters that need open faces are open and those that are closed do get closed. Thus the possibility of confusion is reduced and the difficulty that people have in reading the message is reduced or eliminated.

The upper-grade teacher does not usually teach handwriting as such, but can alter students' sloppy habits by making them conscious of aspects that often lead to illegible writing. Without reminders, students writing may degenerate into noncommunicable scratches.

LOOK-ALIKES.   If *m*'s, *n*'s, *u*'s, and *w*'s all look alike, no matter how consistent the slant of the lines, they will make the script difficult to read. If *i*'s, *e*'s, *l*'s, and *t*'s all look alike, the same is true.

Divide the class into pairs and have the students proofread each other's 100- to 200-word samples and examine easily confused letters. They should underline or circle nondistinguishable letters and write them legibly above the offending letters. Circled words should then be rewritten with an attempt to make the letters clear. One guideline for clear handwriting is to distinguish precisely between letters that can easily be confused. Figure 10.3 provides a sample of a third grader's handwriting, with circled words rewritten.

REWRITING AND REVISING COMPOSITIONS

Rewriting Realities

Students are in the process of learning and therefore are not expected to produce perfect papers. In that sense, there is always something that the teacher can criticize or correct in a student theme. But the goal is to improve, not to be perfect. That places the teacher in the position of constantly providing direction for improvement and praising at the same time that compositions are to be rewritten.

Guidelines on Rewriting

A few guidelines, posted or reproduced for the students, will reduce antagonism and frustration on the question of rewriting. They could include the following:

Figure 10.3
Third Grader's Handwriting Sample

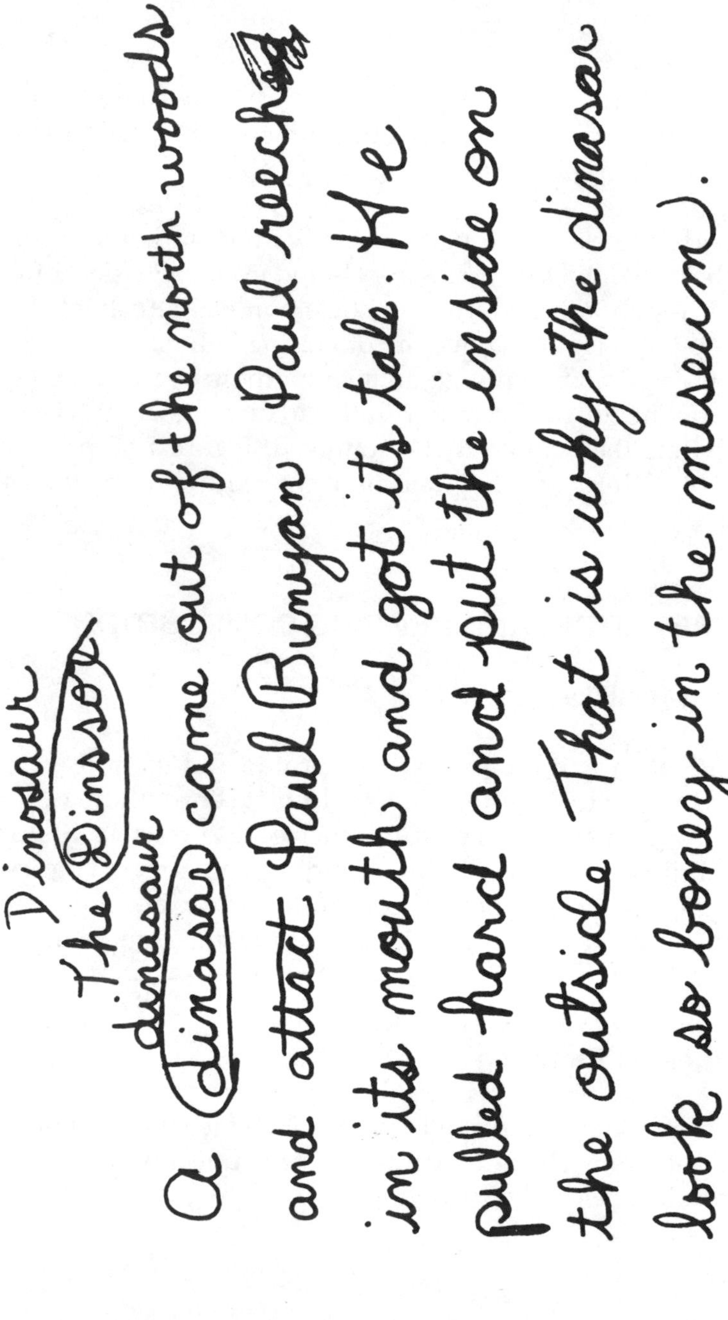

Dinosaur

The (Dinosr)

dinosaur

A (dinosaur) came out of the north woods
and attact Paul Bunyan Paul reeching
in its mouth and got its tale. He
pulled hard and put the inside on
the outside That is why the dinasar
look so bonery in the museum).

1. It is expected that every composition will be proofread—sometimes for a specific skill, sometimes for many things.
2. Any composition submitted to the teacher must be legible.
3. The purpose for and the audience of the composition will determine whether a composition should be rewritten.
4. Some compositions will be graded for spelling, grammar, legibility, and so on, as well as for content. Criteria for grading will be discussed in advance of the submission deadline.
5. Because they are to be displayed or presented outside the class, some compositions may have to be rewritten several times before they are acceptable.

Posted guidelines such as the above keep the expectations clear and help students and teachers through the proofreading and rewriting stages.

How Many Times Should a Paper Be Revised?

Not every composition needs to be revised several times before it is a worthy product. Nonetheless, as soon as it becomes clear that a teacher expects evidence of proofreading, students will get into a habit of revising certain papers.

A Three-Step Revision Process

A three-step process can guide thinking about revisions of important papers.

The first step is a scratch-paper draft just to get ideas down on paper. This draft may be a combined outline and list of thoughts about various points in the outline. It is strictly a personal draft and is not intended for anyone else. It is an attempt to get ideas and language about a topic flowing, and to provide a sense of organization and length.

The second step is an actual draft, the purpose of which is to present ideas in a form that could be shared with a classmate. The classmate reviewer would be encouraged to make notations about mistakes or to raise questions about the clarity or organization of the message. The teacher may also make suggestions on the classmate draft, but it is not to be graded.

The third step is to prepare the composition for a grade or for public display. This is the display draft. Criteria for evaluating this display draft should be known in advance. That gives the student an opportunity to revise according to those criteria and thus makes success more realizable. Some teachers, for example, provide one grade for content and one grade for the mechanics of the composition. Posting the criteria to clarify the content grade and the mechanics grade would be helpful. Other teachers give a single grade, a holistic grade, for a composition and include content, mechanics, and format (sample criteria for holistic grading are given in figure 10.4). Whatever criteria the teacher uses should be explained in advance for the benefit of the student's revision process.

As an instructional strategy, teachers may wish to require that all three drafts of an important paper be submitted together. For those students who experience difficulty in preparing a paper, an analysis of their progression from a personal draft to a display draft might be very helpful in taking corrective action. For other students, the requirement that all three drafts be submitted emphasizes the need for a regular revision process in the development of ideas and in the development of clear writing.

EVALUATING COMPOSITIONS

Students are given grades for their work. Teachers, therefore, need to have ways to evaluate student performance. This book has no easy solution to placing a quality grade on compositions, but we can offer a holistic scoring technique that has worked well for us as a diagnostic tool (see figure 10.4). Coupled with other characteristics that you may want to build in, it may guide you in placing an A, B, C rating on student compositions.

Figure 10.4
Sample Criteria: Holistic Grading

The emphasis in this rating scale is communication, that is, the clarity of the total message as perceived by the rater (teacher). Each scale point represents a description of the kind of communication that has occurred.

COMMUNICATION RATING SCALE FOR ELEMENTARY SCHOOL COMPOSITIONS

Once beyond the first and second grade, the child gains greater fluency in the production of written words. The following criteria on a 1–5 scale provide a teacher with directions specific enough to enable her to rate compositions in grades 2–8. It should be noted that it is necessary for the teacher to define the objective of the written composition before applying the scale. Only after the objective has been clearly determined or defined do the criteria in this scale become valid and reliable, for example, the objective to describe someone's life.

Spelling, grammar, and neatness are not directly considered in this general measure of communication. These elements contribute to effective communication but they need not be perfect to communicate well. Inasmuch as they interfere with communication, however, they reduce the level of the score.

To merit a grade of 4 or 5 the child must demonstrate that he knows how to frame a sentence with a capital and a period, that written language is expressed in the sentence frame, though he may not apply the sentence frame to every main subject-predicate-object unit that he writes.

1–5 SCALE, GRADES 2 AND ABOVE

1: No communication related to the topic or task beyond one simple utterance (sentence) or one idea or a paraphrase of an idea from a known source.

2: Communication related to the topic using several sentences (or equivalent utterances such as run-on clauses) but lacking evident organization. The sentences or equivalents may appear as randomly selected ideas or events.

*3: Communication related to the topic involving several cohesive (organized) sentences, but lacking completeness, i.e., too brief or lacking conclusion.

*4: Communication related to the topic involving a number of cohesive sentences that moves from a beginning, develops the idea, and concludes. A complete and organized statement. This communication would stand as competent because there is a clear sense of sentences as well as a complete message.

5: Same as No. 4 plus originality of expression or idea, or a polished writing style that adds clarity and personality to the communication.

*Some topics, e.g., poetry and lists, should still be treated as messages or communications. They should show order and coherence in order to rate a 3 or a 4. A poem may only have four or six lines but may rate a 4 provided the message is clear and the ideas build cohesively to a conclusion.

Appendix A

WORD PARTS: LATIN AND GREEK ROOTS AND PREFIXES

Recurring word parts can stimulate interest in words and be a way to analyze the meaning of words. A teacher may introduce as a word-generating activity a word part, such as *frat* (meaning brother), and give one example (fraternity). Then ask students to generate other examples and discuss ways the words are used. Some teachers have found it helpful to study five to ten of these Latin and Greek roots and prefixes each week for a series of weeks as a part of their regular vocabulary development exercises.

Latin and Greek Roots

Root	*Meaning*	*Examples*
agri	field	agriculture, agronomy
bio, bia	life, living organism	biology, amphibious, aerobia
capilli	hair	capillary, capilliform
corp	body	corporal, corpus
cred	trust, believe	incredible, credibility
dent	tooth	dental, dentrifice
flec, flex	bend	flexible, reflex, reflect
flu	flow, river	fluent, influence, fluid

Root	Meaning	Examples
frat	brother	fraternity, fraternize
fung	sponge	fungus, fungillis
geo	earth	geology, geometry
gram	letter, writing	telegram, grammar
graph	writing	graphic, autograph
lect	choose	collect, elect, select
lun(a)	moon	lunar, lunacy
manu	hand	manual, manipulate
nat	birth	natal, native, nation
path	suffering	pathology, psychopath
ped	foot	pedal, centipede
phil	love	philosophy, philanthropy
phon	sound	phonics, telephone
psych	mind, soul	psychology, psychical
scope	regard, view	telescope, microscopic

Prefixes

Prefix	Meaning	Examples
ante	before	anterior, anticipate
bi	two	bifurcation, bicentennial
cent	hundred	centigrade, centenary
circum	around	circumvent, circumference
contra	against	contradict, counterculture
dec	ten	decade, decathlon
deci	a tenth of	decimal, decimate
extra	outside	extract, extracellular
inter	between, among	interdict, intercollegiate
intra	within	intramural, intravenous
med	middle	medium, intermediary
mon	alone, one	monastery, monogamy
oct	eight	octagon, octopus
omni	all	omnipotent, omnifarious
per	through	permeate, percolate
peri	all around	periscope, perimeter
post	after	posterior, posthumous

Prefix	Meaning	Examples
pre	before	prenatal, preface
sub	under	subliminal, substandard
super, supra	above, higher than, greater than	superstructure, supramolecular
trans	through	transduce, intransigent
uni	one	unilateral, unify, universe

Appendix B

FREQUENT PHONOGRAMS: VOWELS AND CONSONANTS

Vowels

Five Short Vowels

a (apple)   e (elephant)   i (inside)   o (ostrich)   u (duck)
               ea (tread)   y (syntax)

Five Long Vowels

a (ate)   e (gene)   i (bite)   o (poke)   u (mute)
ay (bay)   ee (keep)   y (bypass)   oa (loan)   ew (dew)
ai (bait)   ea (bean)   igh (high)   ow (know)

Three Variant Vowels

a (all)   o (to)   u (put)

Diphthongs

ou (foul), ow (owl)   oi (oil), oy (boy)

Consonants

Ten Most Frequent Consonants

b, d, f, g, m, n, p, r, s, t

Three K Sounds

k __ (with i or e)   c __ (with a, o, or u)
__ ck (with any vowel)

Soft C

c __ (with e, i, or y: cellar, cider, cyclone)

Three J's

j (jar)   __ dge (judge)   __ ge (change)

Remaining Consonants

h, l, qu, v, w, x, y (yard), z

Digraphs

bl, cl, fl, gl, pl, sl; br, cr, dr, fr, gr, pr, tr; ch, sh; ng, nk; sm, sn,
sp, st, sw, tch; th-voiced, th-voiceless; wh

Irregular

ti (*sh* as in *relation*)
ph (*f* as in phone)
se (*z* as in chose)
gh (*f* as in rough, tough; but no sound in though, thought, sigh)

Appendix C
PHONICS GENERALIZATIONS

The *r* gives the preceding vowel a sound that is neither long nor short: horn, car.

Words having double *e* usually have the long *e* sound: seem.

In *ay* the *y* is silent and is a marker for the long *a* sound: play.

When *y* is the final letter in a word, it usually has a vowel sound: dry.

When *c* and *h* are next to each other, they usually represent only one sound: peach.

When the letters *tch* are next to one another, they usually represent only one sound: catch.

When *c* is followed by *e* or *i*, the sound of *s* is likely to be heard: cent.

When the letter *c* is followed by *o* or *a*, the sound of *k* is likely to be heard: cot.

When *ght* is seen in a word, *gh* is silent: fight.

When two of the same consonants are side by side, only one is heard: carry.

When a word ends in *ck,* it has the same last sound as *k:*   lock.

In most two-syllable words, the first syllable is accented: famous.

If *a, in, re, ex, de,* or *be* is the first syllable in a word, it is usually unaccented: belong.

In most two-syllable words that end in a consonant followed by *y,* the first syllable is accented and the last is unaccented: baby.

If the last syllable of a word ends in *le*, the consonant preceding the *le* usually begins the last syllable: able.

When the first vowel element in a word is followed by *th*, *ch*, or *sh*, these symbols are not broken when the word is divided into syllables and may go with either the first or the second syllable: dishes.

When there is one *e* in a word that ends in a consonant, the *e* usually has a short sound: met.

When the last syllable is the sound *r*, it is unaccented: color.

Appendix D

PHONICS VOCABULARY

ANALYTIC PHONICS. Breaking down whole words to arrive at phonics generalizations.

BLENDING. Pronouncing two or more phonemes as they sound in words. Note: each phoneme sounds different this way than when pronounced in isolation (*stop*, *blast*).

CONSONANT. A phoneme articulated with some closure of the vocal tract.

DIGRAPH. Two or more letters pronounced as a single phoneme (*ea*) or pronounced differently than the sum of the two (*ch*).

DIPHTHONG. A gliding monosyllabic speech sound in which articulation moves smoothly from one vowel to next (*oy, oi, ow, ou*—boy, toil).

GRAPHEME. A written symbol for a phoneme.

KEY WORDS. Words used to exemplify the sound of phonemes (*u* in umbrella, *a* in apple); used in some phonic approach series.

MORPHEME. Word or smallest meaningful linguistic unit (*pre* in preview).

PHONEME. An isolated speech sound (about 44 in English).

PHONOGRAM. Sound produced by *cv* (consonant/vowel) or *vc* graphemes.

STOP CONSONANTS. Consonants articulated with total closure of the vocal tract, followed by release of air (b, d, g, p, t, k).

SYLLABLE. A letter or a group of letters representing a vowel sound or a vowel element, such as a digraph, diphthong, or murmur diphthong. A syllable may or may not contain one or more consonants.

SYNTHETIC PHONICS. Phonics taught for the purpose of synthesizing whole words (adding together sounds: c + a + t = cat).

VOICED. A phoneme articulated with vocal cords (*th* in the).

VOICELESS. A phoneme articulated without vocal cords (*th* in thespian).

VOWELS. Phonemes articulated with no closure of vocal tract (usually a, e, i, o, u, y).

INDEX

Activities
  for capitalization and punctuation, 174
  for composition, 146–48, 149–50, 151–56
  for comprehension, 5, 94–95, 97–99
  for critical thinking, 113–15
    cause-and-effect relationships, 128–29
    comparing and contrasting, 125–26
    distinguishing facts and opinions,
      121–23
    drawing conclusions, 119–20
    making inferences, 116–17
  details, for enhancing recall of, 100–01,
    102–03, 105
  for following directions, 54–56, 136–37
  for handwriting, 176–79
  information, for finding and using,
    141–43
  for linking listening and writing, 50–52
  for listening comprehension and recall,
    47–48
  for motivating reading and writing
    experience writing, 28–31
    literary models, 26–27
    by parents, 24–25
    by teachers, 21–22, 22–23
    through students' interests, 34–37
  for personal experience writing, 28–31
  for phonics, 66–67
  for proofreading and revising, 166–68,
    171
  for recall of information, 105
  for sequencing, 107–08, 136–37
  for spelling, 73–74, 75–77, 173
  for studying, 133
  for summarizing, 109–110
  for vocabulary, 80–82, 82–83, 85–86, 87,
    92
  for Young Authors Program, 38–39
Affixes, 89–92

Capitalization and punctuation, 173–75
Cause-and-effect relationships, 126–29
Communication
  functions, list of major, 9–10
  language arts instruction as, 6–7
  rating scale for elementary school com-
    positions, 182
Comparison and contrast, 123–26
Composition, written, 144–59
  basic strategy for, 148–50
  evaluating, 182
  rating scale for evaluating, 183
  sequence and development in, 150–59
Comprehension, basic, 93–110
  finding main ideas, 95–99
  retaining information, 104–05
  summarizing information, 108–10
  teaching reading comprehension, 93–95
  teaching recall of details, 99–103
  teaching sequence of events, 105–08
Concept diagram, 132
Conclusions, drawing, 117–20
Consonants, phonogram, 67–69, 187–88
Creative writing, guidelines for
    promoting, 22
Critical listening, 56–57
  for complete information, 57–58
  for fact and opinion, 59–60
  for language as emotional or neutral, 57
  for speaker's credentials, 58–59

Critical thinking
  to compare and contrast information,
    123–26
  to distinguish between facts and
    opinions, 120–23
  to draw conclusions, 117–20
  fostering, 111–15
  to make inferences, 115–17
  and understanding cause-and-effect
    relationships, 126–29
Curriculum linkage of reading and
    writing, 6–14
  major communication functions, 9–10
  primary and intermediate grade com-
    munications, 10–14
  target tasks in, 7–9

Description of people, things, and events,
    12
Details, teaching recall of, 99–103
Dictation, 49
Directions
  arrangement of shapes by following,
    135
  following, 134–37
  implementing, 136–37
  listening to, 52–56, 134–35
  restating, 134
Discussion and interaction. See Ideas for
    student discussion and interaction

Error-Reduction Chart, 167
Evaluating and grading compositions, 182
Experience stories
  motivating students through, 27–31
  steps for building, 27
Experience writing
  exercises for, 27–28
  types of, 27–28

Fact and opinion, distinguishing between,
    120–23

Grading and evaluating compositions, 182
Graphemic bases, list of, 65
Graphemic base technique, 63–65

Ideas for student discussion and inter-
    action
  for composition
    speech and written communication,
      similarities and differences, 146

writing process, three stages of, 149
writing process compared with a
    sport, 151
for comprehension
  constructing a summary, 109
  current issues, 118
  identifying main ideas, 96
  importance of details, 100
  sequencing of events, 106
  strategies, 94
  writing a story ending, 102
for critical thinking
  evaluation standards for reading, 112
  motive of main character, 128
about experiences and interests
  observing a court trial, 31–32
for listening skills
  classroom press conference, 50
  evaluating listening habits, 53–54
  "How did it happen?" game, 46–47
for proofreading and revising
  capitalization and punctuation, 174
  notation systems and techniques,
    teacher's, 170
  proofreading team, 165
  spelling patterns and spelling "brain"
    notebook, 172
for reading-writing connection
  summary or concept paragraph, 5
for study strategies
  how to study, 132–33
for vocabulary
  main concept words, 86-87
  word meaning with affixes, 91–92
Inferences, making, 115–17
  instruction in, 116–17
Information location, 137–43
  in dictionaries and encyclopedias,
    138–40
  Guide Word "Gate," 139
  using encyclopedia indexes, 140–41
Information processing for a purpose,
    14–17
  common instructional steps, 17
  levels of processing, 14–17
Interest inventories, 32–33
  pie chart for, 34
  topics of interest to primary and
    intermediate students, 33
  Web of Interest, 35
Intermediate grade communications,
    10–14

Language arts instruction as
  communication, 6–7
Language and concept development, 4–6
Latin and Greek roots and prefixes,
  184–86
Learning centers, 82–83
Learning how to learn, 130–33
  concept diagram, 132
  self-monitoring of understanding by
    students, 131–33
Legibility and handwriting style, 175–79
  group criteria, 175–76
  helping students to write legibly, 175
Listen, learning to, 43–59
  listening experiences that stimulate
    writing, 48–52
  teaching students to listen critically,
    56–59
  teaching students to listen to directions,
    52–56
Listening, the act of, 43–48
  attending, 44–45
  purpose for, 45
  receiving, 44
  remembering, 46
  understanding, 45–46
Logical conclusions, drawing, 18–20

Main ideas
  grouping, by categories, 98
  identifying, 95–99
  sequence of lessons in, 97
Motivating children to read and write
  through experience stories, 27–31
  through interests, 31–37
  literature as a role model for, 24–25
  parents as role models for, 23–25
  principles of, 19–20
  through rewards, 37–39
  by sharing ideas, 39–41
  teachers as role models for, 20–23

Notation system for proofreading,
    teacher's, 170
  alerting students to problem areas, 170

OMAR program, 39–41
Opinions, expressing, 11

Parents
  guidelines for, 24
  as role models, 23–25

Personal experience. See Experience
    stories; Experience writing
Phonics and spelling, 61–62
  graphemic base technique, 63–65
  phonics technique, 65–70
  practice writing and spelling, 74–77
  sound-spelling patterns, 70–73
  unknown words, strategy for, 62–63
  visual sense in spelling, 73–74
Phonics generalizations, 189–90
Phonics technique, 65
  beginning phonograms, 67–68
  ending phonograms, 68–69
  phonograms, 66–67
  practice writing and spelling, 74–77
  using phonics skills, 70–73
  vowels and diphthongs, 69–70
Phonics vocabulary, 191–92
Phonograms, frequent vowel and con-
    sonant, 187–88
Prefixes, 89–92
  Latin and Greek, 185–86
  recognizing affixed words in reading,
    90–91
  word families, 89
Prereading and prewriting, 17
Primary grade communications, 10–14
Proofreading. See also Rewriting and
    revising
  choosing a focus for, 163
  developing a spelling consciousness,
    171–73
  draft and review technique for, 162–63
  getting students to revise, 160–62
  group approach to, 163–68
  strategy for, 162–63
  student responsibility in, 163
  teacher notation system, 170
  teacher's role in, 162
  teaching from student compositions,
    168–69
  team correction in, 164–68

Reading aloud, 21, 24
Reading-writing connection
  clarification of, 1–4
  curriculum linkage, 6–14
  intention in, 17
  language and concept development, 4–6
  major communication functions, 9–10
  primary and intermediate grade com-
    munications, 10–14

Reading-writing connection *(continued)*
  processing information for a purpose,
    14–17
Research and reporting, 13
Revising. *See* Rewriting and revising
Rewards as motivators
  activities for young authors, 38–39
  Young Authors Program, 37–38
Rewriting and revising. *See also* Proof-
    reading
  evaluating and grading drafts, 182
  getting students to revise, 160–62
  guidelines for, 179–81
  holistic grading, sample criteria for, 183
  number of times for revision, 181
  proofreading and, 160–82
  realities of, 179
  summarizing and, 17
  three-step revision process, 181–82
Role model(s)
  literature as, 25–27
  parents as, 23–25
  teachers as, 20–23
Root words, 89–92
  Latin and Greek, 184–85

Sequence of events, teaching, 105–08
Short story
  as target task, 7
  related language activities for
    producing, 8–9
Slow starter, writing activities for, 156–59
Sound-spelling patterns, 70–73
  advanced patterns, 72–73
  graphemic bases, 72
Spelling
  developing a consciousness for, 171–73
  and phonics, 171–72
  and writing practice, 74–77
Student compositions, teaching from,
    168–71
  analyzing sentences, 168–69
  quizzes from student papers, 169
Study strategies, effective
  following directions, 134–37
  implementing directions, 136–37
  learning how to learn, 130–33

learning how to study, 137–43
  writing directions, 135
Suffixes, 89–92
Suggested activities. *See* Activities
Summarizing
  information, 108–10
  and revising, 17

Target tasks (benchmarks)
  description of people, things, and
    events, 12
  evaluation of, 7
  expressing an opinion, 11
  research and reporting, 13
  writing a short story, 8
Teachers as role models, 20–23
  in reading, 21
  in writing, 20–21, 22–23

Vocabulary instruction
  capturing interest in learning, 78–79
  independently increasing vocabulary,
    86–89
  making words easy to remember,
    83–86
  purposes of, 78
  setting criteria for effective planning of,
    79
  using prefixes, suffixes, and root words,
    89–92
  variety of experiences in, 82–83
  through words in context, 79–82
Vowel and consonant phonograms,
    187–88

Words. *See also* Vocabulary instruction
  Latin and Greek roots and prefixes,
    184–86
  strategy for unknown, 62–63
Writing. *See also specific types of writing*
  fostering interest in, 22–23
  sample growth list for, 152
  sequence and development, 150–59
Writing-reading connection. *See* Reading-
    writing connection

Young Author Program, 37–39